met·a·mor·pho·sis

/ˌmedəˈmôrfəsəs/ .noun

1. the process of transformation from an immature form to an
    adult form in two or more distinct stages

There is no end to education.
It is not that you read a book, pass
an examination and finish with education.
The whole of life, from the moment you are born
to the moment you die, is a process of learning.

-Jiddu Krishnamurti

<u>metAMORphosis</u>

Growth Requires Change

.CUSTODIO GOMES.

Also by Custodio Gomes

Life, Love & War
The Human Experience

metAMORphosis

Growth Requires Change

CUSTODIO GOMES

.find your true self.

.for my grandmothers.
Mama & **Malai**
.sempre na nha coração.

CONTENTS

...your journey begins
{NOW}

THE GREAT SELF

Chapter 1

Do you know who you are? Not what you are, but who you truly are. No matter your age and what you have been through in life, you must get to the core of your soul. You must reach within and find out who you are in this thing that we call life. There are many parts of you that the world has yet to see and experience. You are beyond gifted and you have *genius* like talent to offer this world. No matter what is currently going on in your life, you must make time to find your purpose and show them what you want to be remembered for. At this very moment, stop and look at your life with your own eyes, not how the world sees you. I'm sure you have a different view of yourself than what they perceive you to be. Once you begin to self manifest the gift within you, only then will the world begin to see who you truly are. But you must first shed yourself of your past as you begin your *metamorphosis*. Until you realize that you are your only competition, you will forever allow your pride, fears and your *wants* to control you. Remember that no one knows their length of time on this earth, so you have no time to waste. You can not blame anyone else for the choices that you have previously made and the repercussions suffered because of them. You must learn from every experience, good or bad, in order to continually grow into your path. No one is coming to save you, no one is going to bring you to your destination and no one is going to pick you up when you are complacent in life. You must detach from the world sometimes, so your blessings can come into play. As the saying goes, "be in the world and not of the world," if you have desires of conquering any of your many dreams. I know that sometimes we all get caught up in our family and friends' affairs, but those are minor distractions that can hold us back from achieving what we desire. Those whom are successful have learned to constantly keep moving, no matter what the circumstances are. You must be willing to sacrifice your social life, your sleeping patterns and/or whatever comes to distract you. Remember that we all have 24 hours in a day; so what you do with yours, will determine your rewards.

so...WHO ARE YOU?

There are many of us who are just *okay* with surviving. Most are content with getting up, going to work, paying bills, raising the kids and complaining about it every single day of our lives. Many of us don't know what it is to live versus just existing. The fear of failure is the greatest component that keeps many from taking a chance and leading forward with just faith. The lack of courage to go after what most want in life, keeps many souls at bay. Do you know what else keeps many from reaching their dreams? Discipline! Many people can not take a loss, so they quit in various stages of their journey because it becomes too hard. But have you ever asked yourself what your calling is? What you have been put on this earth to do and how it will be used to influence humanity. Sometimes you have to just look at your job and know that you were not put here to do just that. Everything that you go through is a testament of your strength. All tribulations are created to make you more aware of how resilient you are and that you have a great calling in your life. From the first breath that you took, to the last one that you will take, know that you are here to inspire. There is no such thing as coincidence and your Creator doesn't make any mistakes. The calling in your life is fully aligned with the gift that you were born with. Sometimes many will say, "I don't have a gift because I have no talent," which is the greatest disservice to your Creator. I am sure that you always feel it inside, no matter how long you have ignored it. Know that it will never go away because it is part of you; well until you decide to unleash it unto the world. No matter what anyone says, you must always follow your intuition and go with that *gut feeling* that forever awakens you in the middle of the night and in times of despair. Your life will never be complete until you take heed to your calling. It will forever torment your spirit and ignoring it will only cause you to live a mediocre life. You will never be fulfilled with whatever you choose to replace it with. There is no *right time* to listen to your calling; the longer you wait to put it in gear, the longer you will be stuck in misery. So how long are you going to disregard the only thing that brings you endless happiness and inner fulfillment? Today, I implore you to please stop wasting your talent and get to it.

so...**WHAT IS *YOUR* CALLING IN LIFE?**

Let me see that smile. I don't mean that smile which someone temporarily puts on your face because eventually those always fade away. I am speaking about the smile which shows the world that you love yourself beyond all measures. There is a love within you that no one should be able to tamper with. A place of love that you can go to whenever the world becomes too much to handle; so you shut down and run to that special place. Don't get me wrong, it is beautiful to feel loved by others, but sadly that love comes with stipulations and conditions. I'm referring to the types of *loves* that are usually more painful than pleasurable, which causes one to question if it really is love. I want you to reach inside your beautiful soul and tell me what you have done lately to show yourself that you *really* love yourself. It has nothing to do with material trappings, but greatly to do with spoiling your spirit. One must remember that real love comes from within and from emanating what we all have been given. There are many who seek love from outside sources and various frivolous things in this world. Once the realization of self love embodies one, then the simplicities of life are appreciated. You can not offer yourself to another being and expect that they will love you, as you love them. Love has no expectations or any benchmark to determine if it is mutual. You can not give if you are unable to provide yourself with what others require. Many who are unaware of this reality usually place such burdens on the people who are in their lives. The realization of this notion will bring you infinite happiness and it will help you self-evaluate the love that you owe yourself. Many say that the world is a cold place and that you must guard your heart at all costs, but I disagree. If one loves oneself, then that self-love has the ability to powerfully enlighten the world.

You, yes you have the ability to heal many, but it must be done with genuine love and compassion. This can only be attained if one is true to oneself and practices genuine love before stepping out into the world on a daily basis. The word *love* has been distorted and perverted to no end; the world needs more lovers of humanity, rather than fighters who tell us otherwise. It all begins within oneself, before one can ever think of inspiring others to follow one's lead.

so...**HOW MUCH DO YOU LOVE YOURSELF?**

They are not you and you are not them. Comparisons have never done anything for anyone other than stagnate one's progression. Life's lessons at times may come from affiliating yourself with *them*, but it will never make you whole. Many look at others and wonder why one is not in the same position as others. But you must remember that everyone has their own battles to fight, pilgrimage to take and mountains to climb, in order to reach one's destination. You are unique and have certain talents that no one else has. There is no specific time as to when you will arrive at your destination. *They* don't know what you have been through and you don't know what they had to do to gain the blessings of their lives. Measuring oneself with others is a waste of time and it never achieves anything. In retrospect, it actually takes away from your greatness and places a strong emphasis on others. One must learn to walk on one's own pace; attempts to chase another's success will only slow your personal progression. Envy and jealousy are the enemies of your God given talent. You must learn to walk on your own pace, perfect your God given talent, without staring at what others are doing and achieving. Always remember that you have a unique soul. Your beauties are yours, your feelings are yours, your weaknesses and strengths are yours and your roads are meant to be conquered by *you*, not them. Once comparisons no longer come into play, you give power to a universe that offers everything. So what you put out into the world will eventually come back tenfold. Your thoughts, actions, executions or lack thereof, are what you are reciprocated with. So watch how you view the world and be careful what you exhale because it will inevitably be what you inhale. When people say that you are talented and gifted, make sure you take it as a compliment and never shrink yourself to allow anything or anyone to determine your blessings. Many will inspire you and others will question you, but never make the mistake of allowing anyone's words to define you or what you stand for. You are the captain of your own ship, the master of your own destiny and the leader which you previously sought out in others.

SO...WHAT ARE THEY TO YOU?

On the road to a greater life, there will be many required sacrifices. The main issue with many of us is that we don't want to give up things that we love *and/or* things that we feel we deserve. Pride is a very powerful deterrent to one's dreams. Sometimes we may feel that we know it all and feel that we can continue doing the same things, in attempts to reach greater destinations. That is the ultimate mistake. In case you were asking, yes you will have to remove some people and certain things that you do in your life, in order to get to where your blessings await you. One of the most challenging things to do in life is to invite change, knowing that it is necessary for growth. Most people refuse to change their ways, yet constantly complain about their lives. You have to make a decision and stick to it. What you used to do in the past will no longer propel you into the greatness that awaits you in the future. Friends, associates, party partners and even some family members will have to be let go. Remember that not everyone cheers for you, unless they can benefit from you. Once you understand this concept, regardless of how hurtful it is, you will begin your journey to self-liberation. You can not and must not give any energy to anyone who speaks negatively of you, berate you or belittle your name when you are attempting to grow into whom you were created to be. Understand that those closest to you are usually the ones used against you. Your heart must never be your weakness because love is said to be the greatest weapon of manipulation. Beware of false smiles, weak hugs, soft handshakes and limited conversations; for they are all signs of disloyalty. Discernment is the greatest tool given to us. If something looks or feels out of order, then most likely it is. Never betray your intuition, in any situation, when it does not feel right in your spirit. Never hesitate to ever leave behind anything that comes to distract your ambition. Those are vital signs which you must take heed to or be consumed by. I will not lie to you and say that they will not hurt, but the lessons learned are what will help you progress in your path. So keep going, only look back to see how far you've come because the glory that awaits you is far greater than anything that you have ever imagined.

SO…**WHAT ARE YOU WILLING TO SACRIFICE?**

Many people are afraid to speak up and show the world their worth. I need you to know that if you don't speak up for yourself, then the world will gladly tell you how much you are worth. Wake up everyday knowing that you are priceless and that the world needs your input. You must never shrink yourself in order to *not* outshine others. You have worked too hard to reach the level that you are in and it would be a shame to see you make yourself smaller, in trying to not offend others. Your stature was meant to be great and enormous, so others can be in awe and inspired by your work. It is not a sign of conceit, but a form of confidence and humility. Have you not lost endless sleep, worked until exhaustion and sacrificed so much to get to where you are? If so, then why are you hesitant to shine? Be bold enough to show the world the beauty of your soul, so they know that the essence of your presence is a gift from your Creator. Limiting yourself will only stop the world from growing. You must remember that the knowledge you gain, the wisdom you possess and the life you decide to live, will only serve as a guide for those that you come across in your journey. Stand tall, smile with conviction, speak with relevance and walk with confidence so they know who you are. There is no point in stepping into a room and hiding from the crowd, due to a lack of confidence. Let them know that you have arrived, that your voice needs to be heard and how your presence needs to be acknowledged. Be knowledgeable on various topics and always listen to learn with the greatest intent. In life, we learn from everything and everyone, so it is vital to have an open mind. The acceptance of any other's light will only enhance your own presence and value. Remember to swim away from the tide, so you can stand out from any crowd that tends to follow trends. Once you finally make your powerful existence known to the world, they will acknowledge your appearance and know that you came to shine and not dim in any way or form. Your presence is a present; always know and believe that.

so...**WHAT IS YOUR WORTH?**

Many of us are guilty of this. We look at our own lives and we compare it to others that are doing *better* in life. We easily lose focus on the blessings surrounding us and place more emphasis on the monetary gains of others. This creates endless damage to our psyche and disrupts the road that we're attempting to travel. It can also bring added stress and anxiety, which can stunt one's spiritual growth. You must take a step back and realize that you do not know what people have had to overcome in their personal lives. I am sure that there were numerous sacrifices made, which many of us will never experience. We all lead different and contrasting lives. Comparing yourself to anyone is diminishing all of the work that you have done and it also puts a time limit on achieving your own goals. But dreams have no limit; they also have no time expectancy either. You must work to perfect them every single day and never give way to complacency. Stopping to stare at the beauties of what others have attained will only cause you to become undisciplined and distract you from where you are going. Sightseeing is beautiful, but it is only there to remind you that you have much work to do and much to accomplish. If you ever find yourself in comparison to any one else's blessings, just kindly ask them what did they have to do, in order to reach their destination. But most importantly ask them what they have done to remain at that great level. Blessings come in different forms, for different individuals, who are doing different works. So tonight when you have some free time, sit in front of a mirror and just analyze yourself. Ask yourself: what are you doing *consistently* to reach the goals that you previously set for yourself? Use other people's success as inspiration and not as a measuring stick. As long as you remain focused on what you have to do and not what they are doing, then you will be just fine. The blessings showering down on others await you as well; you just have to continue on fulfilling your own calling and the acknowledgments will eventually come.

SO...**NEVER COMPARE YOURSELF TO OTHERS**

Change. It is what many people are looking for, but have much trouble accepting. A change for the good, so they can build a better life for themselves, their families and their communities. But there are many things which need to be evaluated before any change can take affect. I believe that one must first know *what* one is gifted with. Understand that your gift is something that you are great at doing, without exerting much effort. Most people tend to chase *many* different dreams, which bring them no passion or inner fulfillment. You must be real with yourself and know what you're really talented in. Once you realize this, you can focus on what you want to do with your life and learn to perfect your God given talent. You must be realistic in both your short/long term goals and never deviate from the task at hand. Yes distractions arise, but it is up to you to decide how you are going to react to them. Many of us tend to remain in certain situations and/or relationships that have long outgrown us. You must learn to see the signs of life and know when it is time to move on; when the lesson has been taught. Remember that nothing is ever a loss and every situation presents an experience that only life can provide. Be real with yourself when it comes down to any relationship in your life; either romantic or platonic. We all know that expectations are the precursors to dis-appointments, but *you must never* lower your standards. People will only treat you as you allow them to. You can not complain about how you are treated when you lower your standards to a meager level of disrespect. Be real with yourself as to what you are willing to tolerate and know when you should stand up for yourself. Many people claim to have a 'zero tolerance' demeanor, but behind those private doors they dare not openly speak their minds. Remember that the world will always be judgmental, regardless if you're doing good or bad, so just be yourself. Lies about you will only come to disrupt your hopes and dreams; especially when accepted by the self. Starting today, I want you to be boldly honest with yourself as to how you are going to achieve everything that you have long procrastinated. Finish reading these words and get to it!

SO...ARE YOU GOING TO BE REAL WITH YOURSELF?

PERCEPTION

Chapter 2

There is so much noise out there because humanity has turned away from being humane. We awaken everyday to negativity in the streets, in the news, on the lips of many and it inevitably takes a toll on our souls. Many speak negatively about those who are working tirelessly to make this world a better place for all. But at the same time there are many who sit by idly; doing nothing to bring change and refusing to speak out against injustice, due to fear of retribution. It is a specific form of fear that causes people to choose between opposing sides of patriotism. But what many do not understand is that patriotism should always come second to humanity. We are placed here to be loyal to each other and not fight for those who seek to expand their powers through border wars. So you must find the strength to be courageous enough to swim against the tide. Sometimes it can feel as if humanity is against you, but you must never give in to any kind of pressure. No matter what part of the world you live in, you must be bold, strong, brave and outspoken whenever you see other beings suffering. Understand that *they* may eventually come for you. They will drag your name through the dirt, research your past and try to use it against you. They will belittle your courage and mission, then paint you out to be the enemy of humanity. You must prepare your heart, strengthen your mind and know that the toughest battles come to those who attempt to shed light on the world's corruption. But I must warn you, it is very lonely and you may suffer much. Those around you will also be attacked, as a ploy to break your spirit and force you to abandon your task. Many will eventually break down, give in, throw in the towel and abandon what they first started. But on the other hand those who continue on, become legendary and their names are plastered in books for generations to come. But it is all up to you, it is your choice. Either you are going to be remembered or your name is going to vanish like many who quietly passed through this place that we call life. As the saying goes, "don't tell it, but show it" with the actions of your life.

HUMANITY vs YOU

"The quality of being able to grasp or comprehend what is obscure." That is the definition of this powerful word that many people tend to ignore or disregard. There may be many things in this world that you will come to ignore, let *discernment* not be one of them. Many are quick to speak their minds, but they tend to only listen with the sole intent to just respond and not comprehend. When they respond, it is usually with comments that are laced with passionate disdain for what they hear; and not what they listened to. Understand that if you do not pay attention and listen intently to what others say, you will disregard the power of discernment. In order to have a full grasp of your surroundings, you must pay close attention to what people refer to as the *gut feeling*; which is actually your intuition. Intuition is the voice within you that clears the debris off of life's struggles and makes way for you to quickly reach discernment. It paves the road for what and how that *voice* within you is always trying to direct and guide your steps in life. Once you have that *gut feeling,* you will easily learn to decipher what people are trying to say or do. You will gain an advantage that many fail to use, when addressing the issues of life. But there are repercussions for ignoring your gift of discernment. Once you ignore this precious gift, you will work in the flesh and not in the spirit. Meaning, you will stunt your own spiritual growth and continue to do what did not work in your past. Before acknowledging the gift of discernment, one is unable to comprehend what is happening in one's life. You may have blamed others in the past for what you struggled with. But once you gain the true comprehension of discernment, you will be able to analyze life with a broader perspective. Accept your light and you will no longer dwell in the world's darkness. Once you submit yourself to this beautiful blessing, then life becomes much easier to navigate. So it is up to you to finally tap into this power that is freely given to you or you can choose to continually ignore it. All you have to do is stop, listen and feel it become part of your being.

DISCERNMENT...is a gift!

What could be more beautiful than the understanding of the self? Maybe it's just me, but I have previously found myself in the craziest situations (multiple times) in life and knew exactly what to do because my understanding of *the self* saved me. They do say that repetition makes perfect and I must admit that I have had plenty of practice. It is of the greatest tragedy to go through your entire lifespan and never grasp the importance of self-understanding. Just going through life nonchalantly and being content with only surviving is a detriment for anyone. Maybe it is just me, but I want to live my life by experiencing it to its fullest potential and constantly learning the boundaries of my soul. I also want to learn when it is time to slow down, when to be quiet and just enjoy a peaceful silence. I believe that self-awareness will bring everything to me because I have learned to accept what is meant for me and shun what may come to harm me. Knowing one's limit will bring enough *thrill* to satisfy this hunger of ours and constantly keep us connected to others. No matter what is going on in the world, your reaction will always reflect your perception. If you do not understand the dynamics that rotates this earth of ours (political, cultural, spiritual or economical), you will forever be angered by what you see. How you intake information determines how you react to the world. Remember that every action has a reaction and the understanding (or misunderstanding) of your own emotions will always determine your response to it all. The opinion of others should never dictate your behavior because you are solely responsible for how you choose to carry yourself in the world. You will be judged by your actions and no one wants to hear that he or she *made you do it*; especially if you claim to be an adult. Excuses are for the childish and immature, so unless you want to remain categorized, I suggest that you tend to your own mindset. Growth is required for change to take effect and expectations will always be placed on you by the world. So in retrospect, it is always in your hands to make self-awareness a part of your healthy diet; especially if you are going to be in the public eye. You must learn to always check yourself, regardless if *they* are watching or not.

SELF AWARENESS is a must!

Can you please step up closer to the microphone? Those of us sitting in the back are unable to hear you clearly! Remember that you have a responsibility to speak up against any injustice that you see in the world. For those of us who work for the betterment of humanity, we would like to see you put the *human race* before your own race and color. We are all on this journey to become complete human beings, before we are returned to our creator. But how are we to achieve this massive goal? How can we shun our own prejudices and view the world as one single family? It all begins with empathy. Empathy for those who hurt, for those who suffer under ruthless leaders, for those who are affected by the loss of their families and/or for those who lose their own lives. You must reach within, far back to where society has not yet affected and pull out the real you. The *real you* which stems back to when you were born and saw humanity for its innocent possibilities. Innocent and pure without the tainting of society or the added prejudices that are influenced by family members and friends. Reach back to when you defended your *urban* friend from those who did not want to include him in the games you all played in elementary school. How about you reach back to when you confronted your friends for making fun of you because you constantly partied with that *specific* kid from the *suburbs*. Once you find that person, hidden deep within, I implore you to confidently walk up to the microphone and give them nothing but the beauty of your soul. Courageously speak out against the things that you see going on in the world and everything that doesn't sit well in your spirit. Speak with no fear, regardless of how some may disown you, curse you, call you a sell out and refer to you as a race traitor. Stand up and fight against those who continually spread hate and always make sure that your voice is heard. Remember that those who seek and accept separation may be suffering from the same thing that you once suffered from...fear. I am speaking about the fear of becoming an outcast, the fear *that* they will no longer love or care for you because of your outspoken stance. But you must take into account that speaking out, may also bring out a positive affect. It may bring together those who are lost, those who are hateful and scared, as well as those who wish they could be as courageous as you. Never forget that your ultimate goal in this life is to bring people together by inspiring them to take a leap of faith and to have a belief in the power of love and humanity.

so...**SPEAK UP and SPEAK OUT!**

One of life's greatest challenges is figuring out what is more important to you. The struggle between equity and equality lies heavy on the conscience, when faced with the state of the world. Many of us are afraid to voice our opinions because it may eventually affect our funds. In other words, some remain quiet because many believe that speaking out against the inequalities of the world may cause them to lose their jobs and/or source of income. But perception is based on the understanding of the self and one's personal connection with the world, regardless of our cultural or racial differences. One must understand that we all have a responsibility to fight for one another, whenever we witness the mistreatment of anyone. The world can not afford to have you willingly silence your disagreement and disapproval of others who may be suffering. You have to be courageous, while knowing that most may not agree with you in making such a necessary and selfless decision. I respect and understand the need to take care of one's family, so I am fully aware of the difficulty of making this decision. In order to bring change, you are required to be in the *game*, even though most don't get involved unless they are personally affected. You must comprehend that it is of the utmost importance to boldly raise your voice against any wrongdoing that you may come to witness. Sitting there and just complaining to friends and family is not enough to bring change. Remember that silence is another form of complicity, especially if you vehemently disagree with those who are responsible for the oppression of others. If you remain quiet, then you are just as guilty and your conscience will forever remind you of your refusal to defend those who are being oppressed. So take a look in the mirror and ask yourself if you're going to be a champion of peace for all people or are you just going to be a coward who fears the repercussions. But know that they will eventually come after you, due to your outspoken disapproval of the mistreatment of your fellow human beings. Everyone wants to be remembered for doing something great in their lives, so why not just create your own legacy by fighting for those who are unable to defend themselves? Never forget that you are here to fulfill your calling and help others while you're at it.

so...it is **EQUITY vs EQUALITY!**

The main point of learning about the self is to be able to hold your own in life. Sadly we all live in a cold world which tries to do everything to break you and make you succumb to the struggles that you encounter in life. But you must be strong, not a cold hearted kind of strong, but build an inner strength to always fight for what you hope to achieve in your lifetime. Understand that you are going to fail many times, you are going to be embarrassed as well, but your strength to overcome adversity is how you will always be judged. Accept that the mistakes you make, the many times that you fall and the scars you accumulate will be necessary lessons that will propel you to your greatness. Know that those who reached greater levels in their lives are those who never gave up, they are those who held their own and were able to passionately embrace the many lonely late nights, followed by early mornings. No one is coming to save you and truthfully no one is supposed to come save you. God gifted you talents, as He has equally gifted others and you must know that we are all different. But your *difference* doesn't separate you from humanity; it actually brings you closer together. You are not the first person to stumble and fail; for you will not be the last. We are all tested daily and all are judged by society for how we are able to rise after the initial fall. You must know this, embody this and embrace this wholeheartedly if you are serious about the dreams that you continually brag to your friends, family and closest confidants about. You must come to grips with the truth that not everyone is going to support you and not everyone is going to cheer or clap for you. You must learn to be your own cheerleader. Even when you don't feel like working on that gift; you must make yourself rise because nothing is going to change for you if you don't change your ways.

You may struggle, but keep pushing because no successful person had it easy. If anyone tries to show you an easy path, ignore them and take the path less traveled because you will greatly appreciate the learned lessons. That pain will make you value your success much more than the easier traveled road. Always know that your future depends on you and no one else.

so...**HOLD YOUR OWN!**

We are all students of history and we are learners of past errors. We are all well aware of what occurred through time and how people suffered for the advancement of a few selected nations. Civilizations have been built on the backs of many in order for those of an elite class to continually prosper. War is money. There is no other way around that truth and those who disagree with it tend to usually be on the prospering end of this notion. There is a famous saying, "war is an old man's dream and a young man's nightmare" and I couldn't agree more. War has been the greatest tool used in humanity's separation of race, color, gender, class and creed. Subjects are turned into objects, so killing becomes the norm for the justification of the individual's actions. Nations that claim to be *world powers* have built their empires on the subjugation of other vulnerable countries. There is no glory in war, but only death to those who lose the battle and the potential affects of post traumatic stress disorder for the victors. Those who have been said to have committed unspeakable atrocities. Society will try and tell you otherwise, but there is no way around this truth. Propaganda is used to advance the agenda of all nations who *claim* to fight for the freedom of all; but usually have an ulterior motive behind their *war* for peace. Evil begets evil and love is the only antidote. Peace is the only way to live in harmony with one another. The need to protect one self is a God given right, so I am not challenging that fact. Yet we must learn to find a way to coexist and bring world peace to all inhabitants of this beautiful earth. Some people may say that world peace is an impossible feat and that the world revolves around wars; yet I beg to differ. We all have freedom of choice; therefore peace can only be attained by accepting the fact that there is no credible evidence to suggest that there is any real difference between any of us. The problem is the implementation of patriotism (within all nations) that has been misused to convince others to kill in the name of their birth land. But imagine if we all had world citizenship, respected each other's religions, celebrated one another's skin color, practiced equality for both genders and had an acceptance for all races? We can not afford to continually make the same mistakes as those who came before us. We must go a step further and challenge those closest to us. See, the easy part is confronting and attempting to change the perception of strangers. The difficulty lies in speaking to those who are closest to you; those who may feel more comfortable in spewing their separatist and racist hate around you. Never remain complacent; challenge them and challenge yourself, at all times.

SO...**PEACE IS THE ONLY WAY**

No one is perfect, we are all human. Understand that we all make mistakes and sometimes we allow our pride to get in the way of understanding. The problem which keeps us from connecting with others is *listening*. There are many who believe that their opinion is the only truth…when it is just an opinion. Many say that they're entitled to their opinion, which they are, but at the same time they shut off their minds when others tend to speak. In order to progress in life, you are going to need assistance along the way; which means that you're going to have to listen. If you want to attain wisdom, reach the borders of knowledge and flirt with the idea of becoming an intellectual, then you have to learn how to listen and understand. Many of us speak out of emotions and never allow the other person to get one word in. We believe that our opinion is the only thing that matters and if the other party disagrees, then we distance ourselves. I have learned to perfect the art of *listening to understand* and not to just respond. Most of us rarely value the input of others in our conversations. We believe that we must always respond to what others have to say; which can bring tension to the intended conversation. Sometimes all it needs is the removal of self-pride to create a greater connection with another human being. When we listen to respond, we are stating to the other person that their opinion doesn't matter and we are only seeking to counter everything that they have to say. This is what separates the population. Less talking and more listening creates a more peaceful space for dialogue and it also makes others feel welcomed and loved. No one likes or respects a *know it all*. The perception of others is a great thing to have, but the understanding of the self (and willingness to change) is true wisdom. One must be open minded, willing to learn from others and accept them for who they are. There is inspiration within every person who comes into your life, so be careful to not *brush* anyone off. Be mindful of such needed lessons and always listen intently because everyone has something to add to your journey.

so...**LISTEN TO UNDERSTAND**

BLIND EYE * OPEN HEART

Chapter 3

I am black, you are white, she is yellow, he is red, some are tanned, and some are pale...so what's the difference? Can you show me what the color of water is? Better yet what is the color of love? Does your pain bring a different form of suffering than mine? Whenever you laugh, does your happiness differ or contrast from my personal joy? Do your tears flow differently than mine and are they of a different color? I'm sure that you get my point and what I'm trying to relay. There is no difference between you and I. We all bleed red. No child is ever born hating another child because of their skin color, religion, gender or race. That is a characteristic passed down from gene-ration to generation. It is a cycle which some human beings have yet to break. Have you ever taken the time to watch young children play with one another before their parents *and/or* society get the chance to teach them about our potential differences? The negativity and ignorance passed down are what I am referring to. Personally I believe that differences should be celebrated and depicted as beauties of our separate individualisms. Within all of us is the voice of our Creator, so there is no soul is greater than the other. It is a disservice to one's soul to separate oneself and one's children from anyone who doesn't resemble them. Life is too short to bicker about the color of someone's skin, the religion that they choose to follow or the race that they decide to marry; for we all know that love is sightless, touch-less and tasteless. Many believe in the separation of races, perhaps it is because they may still be bitter for how they have been previously treated. As there may be others who blindly and genuinely believe that they are part of a *delusional* master race. But who are you to question the creations of God? And who made you overlord to sanction any separation on earth? The are many of God's beautiful creations which remain untapped due to the fact that many remain afraid to follow their hearts, instead of their worldly teachings. So don't complain about the state of the world, just tap into your own soul; which connects you to every other human being. When fear strikes us all, don't we yell out "oh my God" and when we are physically hurt, doesn't our blood have the same color? There is no difference between any of God's children, only variations of colors within *one* human race. I am quite sure that you know inevitably we all have to return back to our Creator, so be careful how you treat others. For you and I only have a limited time on earth to make a positive impact.

remember...**WE ALL BLEED RED!**

There are many individuals on God's green earth who constantly speak about their dreams and other things which they hope to accomplish in their lifetime. Some of those people believe that such dreams are just beautiful fantasies to romanticize about and don't understand the hard work that is required to truly achieve them. Many believe that as long as you have a dream, you have hope. But in all actuality, dreams without works are infinitely dead. I have come to realize that most people who constantly speak of attaining a certain dream are just constantly attempting to convince themselves. You must believe that whatever dream you have, will only come true if you fully dedicate yourself to achieving it. Once you reach that certain dream, you have a responsibility to help others. Much is given, much is expected. You are given the task of making other people (who can't do anything for you) smile, by offering them hope to reach their own greatest potential as well. But just don't talk about it so much; be about it. It takes much discipline to continually do what you say you're going to do. There are some people who tend to idolize *superstars/celebrities* without knowing what they had to sacrifice, in order to achieve what they have in life. I have always believed that superstars are just ordinary people who chose to fight for and never gave up on their dream. No matter how many times they fell, they never gave up and kept going. They are no different than you or I; they just decided to stick to it and perfect what they were gifted with. We are all gifted at birth; you just have to find yours in your lifetime. We all have the potential to attain everything that our hearts desire in this world. Yet the lack of discipline keeps most people from reaching their dreams, as they continually complain about their lack of achievements. Understand that most achievers are loners (most of the time) and introverts. They understand that their time on this earth is limited, so they don't waste any of it worrying about what others may have to say about them. They are too busy working, to achieve that dream. They have full faith and comprehension that what is conceived in the mind, can be achieved in the physical. Achievers also understand that their gift has the potential to elevate others who may be struggling to find their own calling. But your first priority is to the self and nurturing that talent that *you* have continually ignored since you first felt it. Tap into that gift within you and the world will open up for you. Only then will you elevate yourself and inspire others to do the same.

so...**SAY LESS . DO MORE**

Many say that we live in a cold world, so you must be cold hearted in order to survive. I disagree. Bitterness is the greatest hindrance on one's path towards inner peace and acceptance of all beings. Everyone has suffered or will suffer some kind of separation, disappointment or discrimination in their lifetime. But the weight of hate, anger or bitterness is too heavy a load to carry throughout one's life. You must learn to let go, so you can get to where you are destined to be in life. Some people have a tendency to hold on to such weight and forget that it has the potential to stifle and further delay the blessings that await them. Remember that everyone is fighting a battle that is holding them from reaching the next stage; so be kind and always approach others with an open heart. Sometimes all we have to do is just listen to understand the next person's struggle and help one another in taking that next step forward. There is nothing is this world that can't be overcome; one just has to accept the journey and learn from every single step. There are certain introverts who have the tendency of holding their emotions within and then there are extroverts who choose to spew their problems without any regards as to how others will be affected. But we all hurt sometimes; we all need an ear to listen to or a shoulder to cry on. We are all humans and we all encounter tribulations in life. Some may say that they are okay, yet they are just hesitant to reveal what is troubling them. So know that your approach or reaction will determine the interaction between both individuals. In my lifetime I have learned that misunderstandings at times can cause petty arguments and separation of families, friends or associates. We must remember that opinions can vary when it comes to different topics, so one must have an open mind and most importantly an open heart. Empathy builds relationships and acceptance has the power to heal pain. You may not be the initial source of their pain, but your approach to the situation can determine the connection (or misconnection) with that certain individual. No matter what the world is saying or doing, you must always go with what you feel is right because we all have separate opinions toward specific situations. Remember that you are put here to heal, even when you are personally hurting. Treat others as you would like to always be treated, especially when your mind and heart are in any discomfort. Remember that we all need help sometime. No one is perfect.

so...**OPEN YOUR HEART**

We are all equal children of this place called earth. Doesn't matter what continent we are born in, we all have a stake in every part of the world. The quicker we learn to accept this truth, the better connections we can build with one another. The concept of patriotism and land claims are mere lies created by men, in attempts to keep us all separated. No matter the country you visit, you will come across beautiful souls who will welcome you into their homes. Don't allow anyone to tell you any different. Don't allow world issues and petty quarrels to stop you from venturing out and seeing a world that you may have no understanding of. Many people live their entire lives within their own community, city, state or country and never step out of their comfort zone. So get on that flight that you've long discussed and experience something that you never thought you would. Cultural differences are what can enhance the soul and bring happiness to the spirit. That is the true definition of a blind traveler. One who wants to meet other people (that have no resemblance to them) and see how they deal with their own trials. Remember that you were not put here just to work, pay bills, get sick, discipline your children, complain about your job, be bitter about the life you live and never do anything to change it. You were created to connect with others, regardless of how far they may reside or how scary it seems to just visit lands that are foreign to you. In our early age, most of us partied, laughed and danced with those who have always surrounded us. But don't you want to see how others live? Don't you want to taste foods that you never heard of before? Don't you want to live a full life without any regrets, especially when you are going into your golden years? Remember that a life full of misery, is a life undeserving to live because one's experiences always molds one's understanding of life. So be bold enough to take that trip and take in all of the beautiful wonders that the world has to offer. Your mind was created to see and your heart was created to feel everything. Be brave and leave behind everything that you've known...even if it's just for a weekend.

so...be a **BLIND TRAVELER!**

Racism is taught, no one is born a racist. It is learned behavior that is usually passed down from generation to generation. The world has always had an ugly history with this word. If you suffer from this evil affliction, you should try your very best to rid yourself of this deadly disease. Family and society are the culprits behind the flaming of this fire and we as *one people* should come together to end this epidemic. It may be the hardest action for one to take (when approaching racist friends and family), but it must be done in order for our kids to live in a world that is free of judgment. You may become the scapegoat or the designated *black sheep* of the family, but remember that you're on the good side of humanity; while they remain separatists. Racists are seldom happy because they are always creating scenarios as to why all races should be separate and claiming that race mingling is a sin in the eyes of *their* creator. Which creator are they referring to? Racism was created to keep us all apart. As the people endlessly fight amongst each other, those on top will continue to peddle this lie and benefit from that vicious propaganda. Most racists usually have minimal contact with the race that they hate so much and refuse to see their beauty and humanity. Some have been known to say that certain races are smarter, stronger and faster, yet there is no scientific analysis to back up this concocted theory. Others say that everyone is prejudice in some way, shape or form, but I have to disagree with that assumption as well. Many have been known to use racism to separate religions and/or religious practices. I believe that racism shrinks the person and gives way to the ignorance which has overcome politics, dinner table dialogues and has also perverted the beauty of love. So you have a responsibility to stamp out racism whenever you encounter it. Either if it is you or a complete stranger that is being discriminated against, you must speak up and expose those guilty of spewing their blinded hate. As a fellow human being, you must not remain idle as someone is berated, cussed at, divided, ridiculed or belittled; due to the color of their skin. The endless fight for equality stems from the objectification of certain subjects, used by some as a hidden excuse for their own prejudices. We must never allow anyone, of any race or color, to be treated this way.

RACISM IS A DISEASE

We all have certain destinations awaiting our arrival, but never at the same time. Someone once said that "we should pay attention to those who don't clap when we are celebrated" and whoever said that was absolutely correct. Your present surroundings should never reflect the destination that you are working hard to reach. Your surroundings should be a reflection of your upbringing and the inspiration that will help you reach greater heights. Understand that you are personally responsible for who you allow on your team and how they conduct themselves; regardless if it's a friend, family member or just a business associate. Even though one may be fully focused on one's gift and carrying out the calling given to one's life, there should always be a time of self-reflection and observation of those within one's inner circle. You must understand that we all have *different* gifts and we all reach various milestones at different periods in our lives. It is utterly unhealthy to connect or compare the stage of life that you are presently in and how further along someone else is in their success. You don't know how long they struggled in their journey, how much they had to sacrifice and how many times they almost gave up on their dream. We, as humans, usually judge without any regard to those who are being judged. Envy may creep into our hearts as we look at the outer success of certain individuals. We may be clueless to the inner struggles that others may have wrestled with on their journey. Remember that everyone is fighting something that is constantly attempting to overcome them and success does not exempt anyone from any struggle. So you must learn to focus on your own journey and keep your eyes on the valuable lessons that come from hardships. In time there will be others who may envy you as well. It is futile to ever base your own progression with those who have *made it*; for we all have our own paths to walk. Keep your eyes on your own prize and never envy the blessings that others receive; for they have *carried their own crosses*. Remember that resentment will always be the enemy of one's personal progression. So try to clap a little harder whenever you see your friends, your colleagues, your competition or anyone else that is being celebrated for their hard work and achievements.

so...**DON'T BE A HATER**

Many of us have been known to lose our cool in public, embarrass ourselves and more importantly embarrass our child(ren). When something doesn't go our way, when someone cuts us off in traffic or when we feel wronged in any way possible, our frustration rises to the surface. We forget that everyone makes mistakes and we sometimes tend to lash out without any regards toward our children who are always watching. We are all human, we all fall short of what we tend to preach, but we must never belittle anyone in the presence of those who look up to us (or any other time). We should be a reflection of what we want our children to grow up to be and emulate; so we must watch our ways, our tone and our behaviors, since we expect it of them. How we treat others, display love and compassion will not only set a precedent for our offspring, but also for those we interact with. Many people say that disrespect is the only thing that they will not tolerate, yet some are personally reluctant to offer respect for themselves and others. Expectancy is the precursor to disappointment. So don't expect others to respect your words, if your actions are the opposite. Never have such expectations of your children if you are unable to mirror the exact request. We should always *be* the living standard for what we seek to embed in our children. It is of the utmost importance that we examine ourselves in the mirror every single day and attempt to live up to our words of love, acceptance and forgiveness. This should be consistently done if we are attempting to break generational cycles and raise great young human beings. I know that forgiveness is a hard pill to swallow, but we can not advance in life with the weight of hurt and anger. In our fight for equality for all, we must not be led by bitterness if we are to seek the change that will benefit future generations. We must all teach them (with our actions) to see no differences in any other human; as they will take up the mantle and attempt to continue the fight against those who have long kept us apart from one another. Make sure you're able to walk away from that mirror (every morning and night), accepting of yourself with a clear conscience in all that you do. Your kids are always watching your every word, move and action.

they are… **A REFLECTION OF YOU!**

It is what makes us different, yet unites us all. We are all a piece of a big puzzle and our respective cultures play a big role in making it all come together. Personally I love *cachupa, cannolis, arroz con pollo, hamburgers, bacalhau a bras, general tso's chicken, fufu, brown stew chicken, carne asada, yakitori* or just attending a good *shisa nyama*. I am quite sure that you can figure out that these are all foods from distinct cultures. Most of us love to travel to different lands and try new dishes when we vacation. Collectively we embody the different cultures of the world, but when we return to our own countries, society tells us that we are all different. Those of us who live with open hearts and blind eyes to the lies, fully understand that our love for different cultures' language, music, food and tradition is what makes us all beautifully connected. We seek out people who make our hearts smile, our souls sing and our spirits dance. It may sound cliché but this is the absolute truth. We are open minded enough to live our lives with an acceptance of all souls who are only connected through God's love. We choose to live our lives more abundantly and pay no mind to the ignorance of racism or any other form of separation that has been created to keep humanity at war with one another. We all hold a sacred understanding and belief that every single person has something to offer toward the progression of our planet and we embrace the characteristics of all people who touch various lives. We must quickly defend anyone regardless of their race, gender or color; or anyone who may be ridiculed or persecuted because of their background or origin of birth. The fight within us is meant to unite the world and shun the naysayer who believes that we were created to live in bordered and separated lands. We challenge the hypocrites who eat foods from foreign lands, yet find it in their hearts to speak ill of other countries that don't resemble that of their own. As a great friend once told me, "if you can't change the world, then embarrass the guilty." I believe that this is the only way to ever win over those who are steadily fixated on maintaining the notion that our differences is what will forever keep us apart, rather than connect us. We are one race. The human race.

our are...**CULTURAL DIFFERENCES!**

ACCEPT YOUR LIFE

Chapter 4

Don't fight change. Eventually we are all given the opportunity to walk into our own growth. But the problem is that most people are afraid to be the greatness that they were created to be. Success scares many, as they would rather remain in that safe and comfortable position, which they have been their entire lives. Don't let yourself become that person. Never allow complacency to make you feel mediocre nor get too comfortable enough to continue doing what you have always done in your life. We are all confronted with the possibility of working our way out of our misery, but most tense up and begin to question their own greatness. Well I'm here to tell you that greatness begins in the mind, then it spreads through your body and eventually reveals itself through your works. Many say that "if you put it in the universe then it will be available to you," but the most important component to that quote is the necessary discipline needed in order to reach such elaborate goals. I believe that every single thing is possible in this world. It just requires the *desire* to reach it; an infinite focus and a work ethic like no other. So don't fight it. Don't fight who you are and most definitely, do not fight who you are becoming. One's history will reveal one's past and the great lessons that were taught along one's path. Many people are ashamed of their background, their families and even the place that they come from. But you must embrace and accept everything which has molded you into the person that you have become. You must know that you are great before the world gets a glimpse of you. Remember that you have a unique talent which helps you stand out. You can not become a phenomenal human being (that the world adores and aspires to be) if you don't know your own greatness first. Many say "why me?" I counter with "why not you?" Every single day, you must accept changes that come and embrace every single lesson. Be proud of yourself before the world inflates your mind. Know the beauty of your heart before life manipulates it. Understand your own weaknesses before society has a chance to use it against you. Protect your spirit because they will come question your loyalty and the blinded kindness which allows all others to freely walk in and out of your life. Embrace it all and your path will be much smoother. Remember that the bumps on the road are there to help balance and strengthen you; not to throw you off of your path.

welcome... **WHO YOU ARE** *(becoming)*

First and foremost you must figure out *what* you are struggling with. What is coming to rob you of your happiness and your ambition in life? What stresses you out and how can you learn to let everything take its course? Many of us walk around as if we are stronger than what we really portray. Too afraid to allow anyone in to see how we work and how fragile we really are. The world has taught us to toughen up and to just get through the pain without ever giving ourselves enough time to heal. I read a quote somewhere once and it stated, "...until you heal the wounds of your past, you are going to bleed unto others." That is the absolute truth because one must accept one's past and do everything in one's power to heal before any interaction with others can occur. The past has the power to either liberate or imprison the mind. Denial or non-acceptance will never bring change. We are all human, which also makes us creatures of habit, either for the good or the bad. Most would rather attach themselves to a great memory and disregard the other important factors of their past. This is why many struggle; their refusal to accept the pain, which has the power to keep the mind at a standstill. In order to move forward in life we must learn to forgive those who hurt us in the past. It is not a dismissal of their behavior, but rather a personal release of the trauma caused by the act. It is not done for them, but for you to remove those chains of struggle that have long kept you captive. But like anything else, it is easier said than done. I know that bitterness and revenge is so much easier to latch onto, but the detriment caused to your spirit can not be relieved by anger. It only adds to the pain and slows down the progression that you are in dire need of. Without progression there will be no blessings. The goal is to be a *great/complete* human and to live life in a happy and peaceful state. This can not be achieved if we are continually controlled by the ugliness of anger and hate towards others. Most of us struggle because we have yet to accept the fact that we allow our emotions to control our daily actions. There must be a balance between emotions and logic, especially if we are unable to move forward in life. Whatever past occurrences that may have control over your mind, must be released. Be free and continue to work on just letting go. It will clear the path to a brighter future and you will be free of your mental shackles.

so...**WHY DO YOU STRUGGLE?**

Take some much needed time away from everyone and let this title sink in. It may be a simple title, but most importantly you must understand who *they* really are. The 'they' which I am referring to can be a range of individuals and it all depends on how far you want to go back into your personal lineage. Your crown and your ability to live freely have both been previously paid for with dire sacrifices; with or without your knowledge. People like to say that they overcome the struggles in their life through blood, sweat and tears; but in all honesty, in comparison to history, how much struggle do we really have nowadays? Know that I mean no disrespect nor am I attempting to downplay anyone's struggle. But what do you think your ancestors went through and how hard have your parents worked to make your life easier? Truth be told, we are a spoiled generation of inherited and privileged beings. One must never forget to honor and thank those who came before. When some say, "respect your elders," they are referring to generations of people who sacrificed for you. I'm referring to the people who were never allowed to read and the strangers who challenged the status quo, so you could walk with no fear of discrimination or abuse. Your life is a testament of what they had to march for, were imprisoned for, violently beat for and *if necessary*, many who willingly lay down their lives for. Most nations have had to fight for their freedom, so no one is exempt from this truth. History is not just something of the past, but an important tool for us to reference in order to help humanity continually progress. The sacrifices of the past must always stand for something. So when you walk, make sure you walk with pride, dignity and love for the *kneelers* and *crawlers* who selflessly fought for you. When you speak, you must speak with the utmost confidence and conviction because many who came before you were silenced and not allowed to voice their opinions. You have a great responsibility to honor everyone who suffered for you to be in the position that you are in today. There is nothing more disrespectful in life than behaving as if you're the *only* one who is responsible for your present position in life. Once you honor those who fought for you (without ever knowing you), you will gain an understanding of *how* your own sacrifices will do the same for your children and the future generations to come. Remember the saying, "to whom much is given, much will be required," so you must always remember to *pay forward* what you have received on your life's journey.

because...**THEY FOUGHT FOR YOU!**

First and foremost you don't just represent yourself. Many people have been known to say to their children when they drop them off somewhere, "remember that you are a direct representation of me." Well what else did you think you were? You are a representation of humanity as a whole and part of a bigger picture. Your work, your talent, your gift or whatever you'd like to call it; you're just a grain of sand on life's beach. You are the main role player in your life, in your children's lives and most importantly in the lifetime that you're allotted here on earth. There is no such thing as coincidence, but only God*incidence*. There are no mistakes or inaccuracies; it is all part of your journey. Every action has a reaction and that is why many people point to *Karma* when something comes back to them or others. They say that the universe has a law of attraction (which is correct) but it always has many other laws. Your actions affect everything around you, either if you want to believe it or not. "You reap what you sow" is not just a saying, but the truth in all aspects of life. The actions we take on a daily basis have consequences for days and even years to come. Laws that are enacted or changed, not only affect the present time, but also future generations. You are not just here to have fun, party and pass through life quietly, but to also affect everything that you encounter. We marvel at different architectural beauties and forget to acknowledge the impact that an architect makes on the minds of children who love to design. We argue in public, even scream during road rages, while our child watches from the back seat. Then we wonder why our kids are reprimanded in school for *bossing* other students around. Know that you are part of the bigger picture even if you consciously or subconsciously acknowledge it or not. What you do, forever remains as a remembrance of your life; positive or negative, it is up to you. You are in complete control of your own life and the decisions that you make will determine how people approach you. The position that you find yourself in life is usually based on your previous choices. Never look to pass off the responsibility of your decisions unto society or onto anyone who you may claim to have *made you do it* at the time. Just remember that your actions have the power to affect you and everything surrounding you.

see... **THE BIGGER PICTURE**

Pride is one of the greatest hurdles to overcome in life. Pride keeps one from connecting with others and it also slows down one's own personal progression. No matter what you choose to do with your life, no matter how strong or resilient you think you are, no one does it alone. You must acknowledge and give thanks to everyone who has had a hand in your elevation. You did not arrive where you are today by yourself. Your strength does not just come from you; it comes from the collective people who helped uplift you, since the beginning of your journey. Some of us may think that once we reach a certain status or success in life, we no longer need the help of others. That is a crucial mistake because it will foolishly and inevitably alienate one's support system that is strategically built around that certain individual. Moral support is essential throughout one's lifetime; no one can do it alone. It comes in various forms as well, so you must be attentive at all times and be aware of the blessings that others seldom realize. There are many ways for people to show you love and support you without making it seem as if they are only there to freeload. Your discernment will teach you to distinguish between those who have your best interest at heart and those who are just there for the ride and benefits. There is a daily lesson to be learned and the people around you are not exempt. It matters not if they are friends, family members or love interests; everyone plays a specific role in your path. Remember that most just have a season in your life and they are there to teach you lessons, which will help you get to the next step. But acknowledgement of this and humility within those connections is what builds one's character and growth. At times some of us believe that we can do it all and we believe that we are destined for greatness through our own struggles and perseverance. But eventually we tire out and need the mind to rest a bit. We must realize that there are many working on our behalf, as we take time to recharge our batteries. Make sure that you always choose wisely those you have around you and those who must have your best interest at heart; especially if you're going to place your trust on them. So when you step off that stage and head home to relax, remember to give thanks to the many who have assisted you and played vital roles in molding you into the great success that you have become or are destined to become.

remember...**NO ONE DOES IT ALONE**

There is no such thing in life that comes from a mere coincidence. There is a purpose for everyone that you meet. There are no failed marriages, broken relationships or *mistakes* in your life. It all comes with a price and a lesson that is made to break and rebuild you. Many say that is absolute nonsense and they say this because they may still be angry or refusing to accept the lesson within their specific situation. But can you explain why you keep making the same mistakes? Some use the excuse, "well I like what I like," even though their choices are the reasons behind their detrimental ways. Others justify it by saying, "well they're just stuck in their ways." Sometimes I wonder why many people complain about certain aspects of their lives, yet do absolutely nothing different to change their circumstance. Remember that the destination doesn't have to change, but the path can always be altered. I believe that we all need to learn and *listen* more, instead of just *hearing* what others have to say. There is no justification or coincidence that your heart was broken, even though your main focus is on hating him/her for putting you through such pain. You are not alone, we have all been there. There is no coincidence that your friend betrayed your trust and broke the connection that you two have had for so many years. There is no coincidence that you had such a great connection with that stranger from the train on the ride home from work. Everything happens for a reason and if we don't pay attention, then the lesson may get lost in translation. People are placed in our lives to help mold our minds and help us reach whatever destination we seek. Their words of wisdom or words of hate towards you are vital pieces in building your character. Having expectations of others takes away from what you are meant to receive from them. Whoever *changes* in your presence, to become who you wish them to be, does a disservice to the lessons that you are both required to gain from one another. So it is of the utmost importance to accept people for they are, what they bring into your life and not expect them to become who *you* think they should be. I'm always amazed when people say, "I will become who you want me to be because I love you." That is the greatest disservice to your being. Once that happens, your authenticity may swiftly vanish and you may become nothing but a puppet. So be who you are, regardless of what anyone wants you to be. You are a gift to this world and your beautiful presence was created to impact everyone that you come across.

there is only... **GOD***INCIDENCE*

How you see your life will determine everything. If you are a complainer and always find something wrong, then you are going to have a hard life. Some people see things as half full or half empty, depending on their mindset. A pessimist will always complain, whine and assume what *can* go wrong in their personal life and in the lives of those around them. Their gloomy vision of life will always predict their attitude, demeanor and disposition. Try your best to steer away from those types of people because they are the embodiment of misery. Similar to anything else, misery loves company and can easily fester into an entire lifetime. Be careful of who and what you allow to infiltrate your mind because negativity can have long and dire effects to the psyche. Your mind is your most precious asset, so always try to drench it with daily positives. Instead of thinking what can go wrong, think of the greatness that can come, if it all goes right. Optimism gives hope and offers a very different view of a life that has the potential to be filled with much success and accomplishments. I have always believed that one's mindset determines the outcome of whatever situation one finds oneself in. Seeing the cup *half full* shows that there has been progression and one is half way towards one's goal. It offers hope that anything can be achieved and with consistent growth, the goal is easily attained. Wake up each day with goals and the mindset to achieve everything that you first set out to achieve. No days off. Remember that you are breathing, you are healthy and you have the ability to go after anything you want in life. In contrast to others who are suffering in hospitals, unable to walk or run and endlessly pray to be in your position. Never take anything for granted and always make sure that you are grateful for everything, especially the sanity of your mind. No matter where you are, what situation you find yourself in, know that the circumstance can always be worse. You always have the capability to overcome anything that comes to test you. How you view trials in your life will always determine if you will have a genuine smile or a frown on your face. It determines if you will either be happy or full of anger. Most importantly, it will determine if your happiness is worth fighting for, instead of the misery that the world displays daily. The choice is always yours to make and know that what you decide to pursue in life, will be of your own responsibility and no one else is to ever be blamed for your decisions and choices.

so...**CHECK YOUR MINDSET**

.

It is of the utmost importance that you check on your personal happiness on a daily basis. There are many who constantly complain about everything that goes on in their lives. It can range from work, to relationships, to the car that they drive and the house that they live in. Sometimes we complain, but do nothing to change our situations. So next time you wake up, give thanks for the air that you're breathing, for the function of your limbs and the ability to work and provide nourishment, shelter and security for your family. These are things that we usually don't acknowledge until something goes wrong. We blindly allow the world's stress to consume us and then everything becomes an issue. The whiny child at home starts to annoy you a bit more, the face of that screaming boss seems more agitating, the drive to work becomes endless and all of this affects you more because you're just not happy. Of course we are all going to have challenging days, but our perceptions and reactions toward those days will determine how we are affected. You must learn to stop worrying about the things that you can't control. You can't control the car acting up or the weather being dreary; especially when you finally end that 12 hour work shift. But what you do have control over is your circumstance and your reactions. You don't have to live in that house which you hate so much, hang out with those friends who do nothing but gossip and you also don't have to stay in that dead-end job until you retire and hope to receive a good pension. Remember that everyone has a gift and a dream, so don't waste your time living a mediocre life. You weren't put here to walk through life miserably; you were put here to thrive and live with happiness. You were meant to wake up happy and have enough wealth to live abundantly. Do you believe this notion or do you just constantly question the greatness that awaits you? Are you going to continue complaining and moping around, while the rest of the world's population continually works on perfecting their craft? Remember, it is all up to you. You can watch your friends and family members wither away because they weren't courageous enough to fight for their dreams or you could inspire them. You could also make a decision to finally start living today. Remember that you have to be persistent, patient and consistent if you want to really change your life. By the way, don't worry about the negative friends and family members that you're going to lose along the way; they are just trying to project their own fears unto you because they were too afraid to try anything worthwhile in life. They have accepted their own shortcomings, regrets and misery. Don't you ever allow this to become your life!

so... **ARE YOU HAPPY?**

HUMILITY

Chapter 5

There is a saying that I live by, "humble yourself or the world will humble you." There are many great virtues to live by, but I believe that humility is the greatest one. Pride is the greatest enemy of self-advancement. If you allow yourself to be filled with pride, it will distance you from the people and their ability to see you as an equal. Remember that no person is ever greater than the next, regardless of the success one may attain or the fortune that one may amass. If you separate yourself from the people, then you will have separated yourself from your gift. Most importantly you will have distanced yourself from God and the task that was given for you to carry out in your short time on this earth. In order to become a complete human being, you must not view yourself any different than anyone else. There can be no distinction of color, gender, race, creed or any other form of man made separation. Once you put yourself above anyone, you shrink your own stature within the eyes of your creator. We are all attempting to reach the same destination of peace, regardless of the difference in paths traveled. So, from time to time, you should take a break from your busy schedule, shake hands and converse with various people; learn about them and teach them about you. You will come to learn that there is no real difference between any of us. We all have equal emotions, we all want to thrive in life, we all seek love and happiness, as well as prosperity in our lifetime. Your success should bring you closer to people, instead of distancing yourself further away from humanity. Remember that there is no such thing as an overnight success because we all fall down on our journeys. There is a big difference between those who stay down and give up and those who rise to push forward; for they know that greater things await them. You must know that within you there is a unique gift that will brighten the lives of many and inspire others to find their own gifts. People like to jokingly say, "hey make sure you don't forget about the little people when you become successful," but I have learned that every joke is always laced with some truth. So open your heart, smile more and extend yourself to those who are in need. Your humility is what they will truly remember, love and respect about your character.

so...**HUMBLE YOURSELF**

"It is ok, we all make mistakes." That is what many people like to say that to others, but tend to forget to take their own advice. Some try to disguise it as, "I'm just human" or sarcastically say "sorry but I'm not perfect." No matter how these comments may seem as excuses for someone's behavior, they are actually an acceptance of guilt for what they have done. Know that the admittance of wrongdoing is the first step to one's most important self-elevation. Remember that none of us are experts or perfect; so it is okay to make mistakes and forgive oneself for it. You cannot and must not hold yourself hostage with the rusty chains of past guilt. Guilt has the ability to play on emotions and has the capability to trigger one's anxiety and stress. I've always believed that stress is a waste of time and a weight which I refuse to ever carry. One can't control what has already occurred, but can only learn from its valuable lesson. The pressure that we put on ourselves has the potential of keeping us from reaching our greatest potential. We beat ourselves up for the things that we *should have known* to not do, but without those experiences we would have never reached the necessary levels of understanding. There are many important tribulations which eventually guides us to the where we are meant to be in life. Your parents, coaches, teachers and mentors can only teach you so much; know that your greatest teacher on earth will be life's daily experiences. Rearview mirrors are only there for you to glance and remember how far you have come. But you must never be consumed with the past or worry about what is to come in the future. Life is meant to be lived in the present moment, regardless of the many mistakes that are made or the successes that are waiting to be attained. Some people will randomly remind you of the *craziness* that you did in the past because they are too busy living cautiously and just doing enough to survive. There is no fun in playing it safe, in refusing to *jump* or simply just living in fear of failure. Once you get a taste of life in its rawest form, you will try to do everything that you previously set out to do. So if you scrape your knees or scar your elbows in the process of reaching your goals, know that people will *always* criticize and judge you. But remember to always live your life for you and not for what others may say or think of you.

so...**FORGIVE YOURSELF**

You must learn to appreciate everything and everyone who comes into your life. Sometimes we get caught up in our personal lives and never properly acknowledge the angels that are placed in our paths. I'm sure we can all look back at our childhoods and remember all of the times that we were spared for the mindless things that we did. No one can honestly say that they did everything without any regrets. But as one ages, one realizes that it is all part of one's growth. You learn to appreciate everything that you were able to experience; proud ones and some that you rarely mention. If you believe that appreciation is the gateway to blessings, then you may be absolutely correct. Those who complain are always focused on the negative and what they don't have. Such individuals forget that there are many others who would love to be in their present position. The world teaches us that we need to consume more every day, in order to reach an infinite state of bliss. But the *rat race* towards fame, money and notoriety only creates a false narrative of happiness and peace. One must understand that the journey of life is the greatest gift given to the soul; the destination makes everything worthwhile. The harder you struggle, the stronger you eventually become and the greater wisdom you gain. So be thankful for health, a supportive family, friends who constantly check on you and the supporters who are endlessly inspired by your work. Riches lie within you and those who nurture them for you, are to be forever appreciated and celebrated. We live in a time when everyone seems to only want quick fame and fortune, yet they don't know the responsibility that comes with that. Much is given, much is expected; the more humble you are, the more you are blessed and gifted. So when you awake everyday, give thanks for the air in your lungs, the steady beating of your heart and the ability to walk in health; for there were many who did not awaken today and many others struggling with ailments. Be thankful for what many take for granted. You are blessed and protected with God's grace, even if you refuse to acknowledge it or just don't know of it.

so...**BE APPRECIATIVE**

There are two things that you must learn to accept in life: you are not going to save everyone and you are not to be anyone's punching bag. There are going to be times that you'll need to shut down and know that it's perfectly okay; for you were not created to work without proper rest. We all need our space at times to allow the mind, body and most importantly the spirit to rest. Remember that you are not helpful to anyone if you break down; you must be humble in *your walk* and always know your own limitations. Know that we are all fighting some kind of battle, regardless of how people choose to paint their own *flawless/false* picture to the world. There is nothing greater than a random self-evaluation; for it serves as a daily reminder of what you need to work on in order to help you become a better human being. Yes, there will be people who will take it personal that you may require some space, just to reinforce your peace of mind. They may even speak negatively of you and smile in your face afterwards. But that is okay as well; you must remember that no one knows you, like you know yourself. So if they take it personal, then know that they are not there for your benefit. I know that your heart is pure and you try to do everything with great intentions, but be aware of leeches. No need to further explain anything, when *they* require and expect an explanation. There will be people who will walk away from you because they do not understand what you're going through; you must learn to let them go, as they make their own assumptions for why you are distancing yourself. You must also be strong enough to not take it personal if some of them don't *understand* why you need some personal time to yourself. You may not know it at the time, but those may be hidden blessings; especially when you need to free up some space for self-happiness and more self-love to fill in. As I have stated numerous times before, everything is a learning lesson and your creator places everyone in your life to teach you a thing or two. Never apologize for making room for what is in your heart, regardless of who may have an issue with how you make necessary changes in your life. If they're mad, let them be mad. Not everyone will walk this life journey with you, so don't be too distraught when watching some fall off your path. It is part of life and only you know what is best for you.

always...**PROTECT YOUR SPACE**

When you walk into a room full of people, what is their perception of you? How is your demeanor and what is your perception of them? Traits like this are vital to one's character and it adds to one's ability in connecting with others. No one wants to interact with a condescending and dismissive individual who believes that the rest of the world is beneath them. People should always want to speak freely and confidently without ever encountering the unnecessary arrogance of others. Conceit brings forth a contentious attitude and no one wants to ever converse or interact with anyone who believes that they are better than the rest. So when you dress yourself in the morning, make sure that conceit, arrogance and your dismissive attitude are all left in the bottom drawer of your dresser. Those are ugly traits that stem from the tree of human separation and are inevitably dispersed through the vehicles of one's self-pride. Your roots should be laced with humility and utter confidence. You must learn about yourself and walk with a confident mindset at all times. Speaking with assurance will not only invite others into your space, but it will also attract people who are constantly releasing positive vibes into the universe. There is a thin line between confidence and conceit, so I urge you to check your ego at the door before interacting with others. Confidence is hoping others will succeed and clapping for them, even if they are competing in the same field as you. Jealousy is when you envy others and believe that they may be receiving too much praise for their works, when you feel that you should be *the one* showered with compliments...at all times. Confidence is offering others your light and not expecting anything in return. Conceit is expecting the world to bow at your feet because you believe that you are God's gift to humanity. It is a narcissistic mindset that causes you to believe that others *must* always acknowledge your *glorious* presence. Confidence is offering your generosity and assistance to those who are unable to do for themselves and knowing that they are endlessly grateful. Conceit is the epitome of narcissism and the belief that without you, others will never be great. So I implore you to self-reflect daily, be grateful for life and the air you breathe. Always know that your talent was given to connect you with others; never to keep you separate from those who you are to encounter throughout your lifetime.

CONFIDENCE vs CONCEIT

The main goal in life is to figure out why you were placed on this earth and how you will display your gifts to the world. Nothing more, nothing less. Everything else that you come to experience in life is just additions to enhance your experience while you are here. There are three important days in your life: the day that you are born, the day you learn what you were put here to do and the day you leave this earth. Every single person is a gift to this world and whatever you choose to do while you're here is up to you. That is why we are all given free will. We are all equipped with a unique *genius like talent*, when we open our eyes and finally see our earthly parents for the first time. We all have it. There is no such thing as finding your gift *too early or too late* in your lifetime. The goal is to realize what you're great at and nurture that gift until the world recognizes your brilliant mind. Some people believe that they are not as gifted as others or they may also believe that they have no gift at all. You must disregard those thoughts and learn to curb your mind, so it aligns with the universe. Once you have such an epiphany, you must set high self-expectations and bless the world with the fire that propels you from within. You must never let up, you must not allow anything or anyone to distract you from achieving what you have been tasked to do. In order to achieve the greatest blessings of your gift, you must acknowledge where it comes from and you must give praise to the Creator who embedded you with it. You must remain persistent, patient and consistent on your walk towards achieving such glory. You must also understand that you will be tested, led astray by those closest to you and criticized or ridiculed because the *enemy* doesn't want to see you succeed. But always know that you are called to be steadfast, humble and focused on your journey. Most importantly you must know that you are *not* perfect; for you are just a reflection of the perfection that created you...so accept your mistakes and take heed to every lesson learned. Know that you're always being watched by those who support you and by those who smirk whenever you stumble. You must rise when you fall, admit when you are wrong, know what your faults and weaknesses are, so you can finally persevere. Your life will forever be a reflection of your choices and this is how you will be remembered; as you complete the third most important day in your life. Make sure all is done, before you depart this earth and return to the *One* who blessed you, graced you and made you a symbol for those who you inspired with the gift that you were blessed with.

keep high...**SELF EXPECTATIONS**

No one is perfect. Once you accept this truth, life begins to fully open up for you. Your expectations of others will no longer be disappointing and you will stop beating yourself up for the mistakes that you committed in the past. Many like to say that they are *perfectionists* and everything that they do must always come out perfect, in every way possible. Nonetheless, what you may come to believe is perfection, can also be viewed differently by someone else. One's perception and one's vision is never viewed equally through a set of different eyes. So we accept that all fall short in the eyes of the Creator. You may even see *eye to eye* with some, but your opinions may be different. You may agree on some things, but you will definitely disagree on others. That is the beauty of building friendships and connections with others. Yet most of us like to listen, only to respond, rather than to fully comprehend because we *believe* that our opinion is always fact. You must be willing to accept your own faults, acknowledge when you're wrong and never pass judgment on anyone. In order to build healthy relationships, one must be willing to sacrifice and understand that no one is ever going to *make* you completely happy. Disagreements and misunderstandings arise to strengthen your connection and to teach you how to appreciate the individual; even though you dislike them at times. Love is complex and the acceptance of all faults in someone only makes the bond stronger. You will never be fully satisfied because we are all emotional creatures when it comes to our hearts; especially when we feel that we have been wronged. Sometimes we react without taking into account what the other person is also going through. We are all fighting a daily battle, so we must be careful as to how we speak to and treat others. It matters not if that person is a stranger, family member, lover or just a good friend. An open mind and willing heart can alleviate stress and at the same time help heal others. So be kind, be gentle, be attentive, be forgiving and be a beacon of light because you never know when someone just needs a shoulder to lean on. Remember that *we are all human* and we all fall short of the grace that is given to us daily.

it's okay... **WE ALL FALL SHORT**

In life you're going to come across many people who are going to *do you wrong* and I know exactly how that feels. There is nothing worse than giving someone your trust and they take it for granted or misuse it without any consideration for the pain that it may cause you. I have been on both sides of that equation. I have hurt others and I have been hurt myself. Many people say that's just life and everyone goes through it; nevertheless it doesn't make it any easier to *get over* the pain. Many love to quote various spiritual texts which may focus on the importance of forgiveness. But I will be the first to admit that it is harder said than done. We may share great quotes by *motivational speakers* who claim to specialize in this specific subject, but the question is: do you live by what you preach? Being wronged by someone that you gave your heart and loyalty to makes it that much harder to forgive their transgressions. It takes many years of constant soul searching, spiritual evaluation and self-reflection, to reach the elusive destination of forgiveness. The act of forgiveness is a very hard concept to embrace, but I've come to realize that it must occur in order for one to move on. Holding on to the stains left on one's heart, keeps one from receiving certain blessings. It took me many years to understand this valuable lesson. Being angry only weighs down on the shoulders of the one who refuses to forgive. You can forgive without forgetting because the beauty is in the act. We have all done some unimaginable things in our lives that compelled us to ask for God's forgiveness. So why is it hard to forgive a fellow human for what they have done to us? For most of us, the demand of loyalty and respect makes hypocrites of us all. I am sure that we are in agreement that we aren't always loyal to God; even though He *constantly* forgives us for sinning many times over. Yet we expect forgiveness from our mates, families and friends. So if you don't learn anything else from this chapter, just know that forgiveness is for you, not for the offender. Forgiveness has the power to alleviate the weight off of your shoulders and release the anger from your spirit. There is nothing better than becoming stress free. A long time ago, I learned that anyone who angers you, controls you...and that is absolutely correct. So I refuse to give anyone such power over my being. I choose to forgive with no bitterness, learn from the interaction and move on without ever giving that specific person a chance to afflict me once again. Live, learn and keep it moving.

so...**FORGIVE** as you have been **FORGIVEN**

RELIGION *vs* SPIRITUALITY

Chapter 6

You are worthy. Embrace that concept and know that you are more than enough. You are going to encounter people in your lifetime who will try to diminish your talents and question your abilities, in hopes that they will have power over you. Many say that only God can judge them, yet they allow other people's opinions to define who they really are. We all get down on ourselves, have stressful days and doubts about what we are put on earth to do. That is absolutely normal and that is merely your journey testing to see if you have what it takes to make it over that mountain of doubt. You come from a Creator who gave you a unique and an individual talent to share with the world. Don't be afraid of success, be afraid of not trying. Be afraid of dismissing your talent because the world has become too heavy for you. Don't allow those who squandered their gifts to ever make you feel as if you can't achieve the goals that you set out to achieve. Be very protective of what and who you allow into your spirit. Temptation and distractions are everywhere and they only seem to attack you when you get closer to your goals. Don't run away from it, keep going and only look back to remind yourself of the pain which propelled you to your glory. You have the power to always define yourself; not your friends or family members. In order for change to come, you must be willing to let go of your past ways and shed the people who previously held you back. Worrying about what the critics and *haters* have to say will only feed their negativity and slow down your walk towards the life that you've always desired. Regrets are a waste of time and wishing that your past was different will change absolutely nothing. Your mind must be re-programmed to always move forward and know that your history is just part of your inspirational story. Remember that whatever you have gone through in the past will always inspire those who come after you. So quiet the noise of those who continually say that you will never amount to anything. That is nothing but their self-hate attempting to project their negativity onto your oncoming blessings. Just embrace it, acknowledge it, learn greatly from it and then show them that you have been renewed. Mistakes are inevitable because without them one will never know what growth requires. Self-love and self-worth are your greatest weapons, in your fight to combat and conquer anything that comes to derail you. You are human and you are a blessed child of God, so show the world how beautifully gifted you are.

YOU COME FROM A HIGHER POWER

At times, many claim to be *holier* than others, yet their actions display the opposite. Judgment is only reserved for the Creator, so who are you to look down on anyone? It will only be a disservice to your spirit if you believe that your sin is less harmful than how others sin. But they fail to realize that sin is sin, no matter how small or big we may perceive it to be. You are here to love and heal one another; regardless of anyone's color, race, religion, economic status or beliefs. Many people try to excuse their behavior by claiming that they are *only human,* while invoking the name of their specific savior. There is no difference in the eyes of God; for we are all children of God. No matter where one is born; either if they are fortunate or misfortunate. Eventually at the end, we will all have to answer for how we treated our fellow human beings with our time on this earth. You can not *hypocritically* deny basic rights and equality to another being, while claiming yourself to be a spiritual being. You must never be a hypocrite of *the word*, because He not only sees what we say, but what we do. There is nothing godly about treating someone with disdain, not caring about the poor, speaking ill of those who suffer or believing that God only blesses you. In life we will all fall short of His grace, but we must try our hardest to help anyone in need. Regardless of where we are from, we were all bathed in love before taking our first breath. You may not feel sympathy for what someone is going through, but your heart was lined with empathy before the world taught you to hate. Be careful how you treat people because we all go through challenging times and all need a helping hand in life at times. Your wealth will not shield you from pain and suffering, so be generous by giving to anyone who is in dire need. I know that it's not popular to be open minded and accepting, in a world that teaches us that we must only fend for ourselves and our families. It is okay to speak out against those worldly expectations; it is also okay to rebel against selfishness and to speak up for those who are silenced. You may lose many friends, work colleagues and even family members in the process. You must always remember that your essential goal, before leaving this earth, is to always be a, kind, giving and loving human being. Many excuse their behavior and remain afraid to break their generational cycles. I fully understand the beliefs that you've been embedded with, but if those indoctrinations keep you from showing love and kindness to others then you may want to reevaluate your teachings. I know that everything takes time and we all grow at our own pace, but you must understand that life is about inclusion and not exclusion.

so...**WHAT WOULD YOUR SAVIOR DO?**

Many say that there may only be one difference between world leaders and religious leaders; other than that, the latter is just said to be ordained by God. Ordained to deliver the spiritual word, which is created to help liberate people's souls and draw them closer to God. They are said to be held to a higher standard, with a respective understanding that they are still just human. They are to be forgiven for their transgressions, sought out for counsel and rarely questioned for their actions. But many tend to make them out to be demigods; placing endless faith in them and *offering* them their last currency. Certain religious leaders have taken this power and manipulated their followers into believing that without their approval, the masses will not make it to the glorious after life. Many of these religious leaders fly in expensive jets, live in overly luxurious homes and drive ridiculously expensive vehicles. They are exempt from being questioned and use spiritual scripture to justify their behavior. Many have also stated that "God just wants its leaders to live prosperously," even though their own followers are barely able to feed their families and pay their rent/mortgage. Most religious texts teach that the leader is expected to lead by example, to also prosper *in the word,* but it suggests nothing about living lavishly in this materialistic and lost world. Some in the world have relinquished most of their personal beliefs, which were once bestowed upon them by their spiritual leader. Many others continually follow like sheep, even though they endlessly complain to their friends and family. Regardless of the various documented scandals that constantly ravage these religious institutions, some people still give them a *pass* because they believe that these *religious* leaders are untouchable and holy. But what is so holy about corruption and concealment of molestation within the churches that adorn most corners of our poorest neighborhoods? Religious leaders who would rather protect the man made institution, instead of the masses who placed their faith in them. No one has a right to judge because we all sin on a daily basis and most of us have been known to personally lie to God on a consistent basis. Yet we all have a right to question. Vehemently question the vessel who is supposed to show us the path to a higher power and teach us the importance of humility. Everyone stands before the judge after we depart this earth. But while we are still here, we all have a *human* duty to expect more from our religious leaders and always hold them accountable. It is our responsibility because the preservation of many innocent souls are at stake. We are all expected to lead by example!

so-called...**RELIGIOUS LEADERS!**

In the path towards the almighty, we are expected to respect and love all people. Man created the separation of race, color and religion. Even though no one will ever have an equal experience, we all know that the world's expectation of humanity is on all time low. Religion has become the greatest separation of mankind because many believe that their religion is the *chosen* one. But don't all religions preach love, understanding and acceptance, in return for the salvation of one's soul? Yet when we look out into the world, all that we see is leaders using various religious scriptures to justify their separatist rhetoric. The fundamental cornerstone of all religions is love. Love for those who are in need and prayer for those who come to do us harm. Accept that we all come from different places, yet we are all God's children. The politics of the world now dictates what these religious leaders peddle in their weekly sermons. It matters not what god you claim to worship, but the acceptance of love in your heart is what really matters. Hypocrites will use religious text as a means for personal gains. Religious sanctuaries are used for the benefit of their leaders and not for the elevation of their respective communities. God does want us all to prosper, but at the same time, one has the responsibility and expectation to help the needy and desolate; regardless of one's religious allegiance. If we were to equally accept people of all faiths and religious followings, then the world would become what we have all envisioned it to be. We should all visit each other's churches, synagogues and mosques from time to time and get to know each other a bit more. It would be ideal to share our teachings and our various differences, in order to gain a better understanding of what keeps us apart. Help one another in life because we will all die inevitably and must stand before the Creator.

So from this day on, let us try to be more open-minded, accepting and loving. Let us not just fund the great sanctuaries, but pray more and try to not degrade and attack one another. Let us not be judgmental towards one another because in God's eyes we all fall short. Always remember that what you are taught in your religious studies should make you more aware of how connected we all are. There should be no hate, malice or ill-intentions toward anyone on earth. Don't forget, no one respects a religious hypocrite.

so...no **SEPARATION OF RELIGIONS**

You will never receive anything from this world, until you put in the work to achieve it. We all want happiness, success, financial freedom and even love, but many just *dream* of such things. I believe that many people will never achieve what is in their hearts because they fear the greatness that has always lied within them. Some look at celebrities and wonder why they seem so blessed to live such *great* lives and travel to many luxurious destinations. Some envy them and others just blindly idolize them. The belief that all people can reach great heights in life has become foreign to some because their work ethic will never match their glorious dreams. You must accept the fact that you're going to fall and fail many times before the world learns your name. You are going to stumble, feel like you want to quit and probably be laughed at for your endless ambitions. You have to learn to accept this truth, if you are willing to fully sacrifice and chase after your dreams. The road is never easy, the path is arduous and the rewards may take long to arrive. Nonetheless you must be willing to suffer, be alone most times, while working on your craft. You may even be referred to as being *crazy* for dreaming so big. But you must have endless faith in your talent and know that God will never forsake you, especially when you're giving it your all. Nothing on this earth is unattainable if you put your mind to it, discipline your flesh and keep your spirit away from those who tell you that you will never achieve your dream. Don't allow their misery to kill your hopes; know that their doubts only come to strengthen you. Focus on what you want to achieve, pray endlessly because God hears you and always believe in yourself. It may take longer than expected, but know that all will come to you on its designated time. There may be many others who seem to always thrive, but keep in mind that you don't know how long they had to struggle before reaching their blessings. You must relentlessly work on your craft; for life is not going to gift you anything. Doors may be shut, but your prayers will be heard when your works are consistent. You must also know that your pace must never be compared with anyone else's, regardless of how long it takes you to achieve your goals. I have no doubt that you will indeed reach your goals. Your heart is pure, your intentions are genuine and hard work will always beat lazy talent. So treat every project as if it is your first, always embrace humility and know that your kind heart will always be appreciated. No need to keep speaking about your dreams, just work hard, reach them and then allow your success to speak for itself.

so...match your **PRAYER AND WORKS**

Everything you do and everything you are comes from your Creator. Don't believe me? Then answer me this: what is the first thing you say when you're in trouble? Is it "oh my God," or is it something else? Look at your life, look how you overcame your struggles, look how you've become a blessing to many people, look how gifted you are. Many of us are used to doing without thinking, that we sometimes forget to be grateful for everything. In the past when you attempted to do great things on your own way...did it not fail? When they ridiculed you, laughed at you and attempted to harm you, God came to your defense and made you a shining beam for those exact people. We are all human and pride is one of our greatest faults because we believe that we create our own opportunities. The glory is never yours to claim because the grace didn't come from you. So when you do well and the world glorifies you, make sure that you correct them and remind them who the glory belongs to. You don't have to be part of any specific religion to feel when your intuition (which we call a gut feeling) is telling you who your enemies are. When we enter this world, we are all embedded with a special and unique gift to help us navigate through life. That gift is polished to perfection and then presented to the world as a reflection of your Creator. Let no one tell you differently, especially those who fail to accept their own gift in life. We are all geniuses and have the ability to connect with God. When you say your daily prayers, make sure to give praise and be thankful for everything that you have experienced. I know it's not popular and sometimes you get too busy, but make it possible once you realize it. Be careful of those who come to steal your gift with false smiles, hidden grins and monetary bribes. Never build with anyone who is a slave to the world; take heed to your intuition and never disregard your gift of discernment. So if you refuse to live a mediocre life and seek to live abundantly then build with God, and His grace will open doors that you would have never thought possible. It is all up to you and it is the main reason why we were all given *free will*.

so...**BUILD WITH GOD**

When you pray, do you only pray for loved ones and friends or for strangers as well? Do you include the homeless, the hungry, the stressed, the destitute, the poor and the rich; the ones that you will never come to know or meet in life? Have you ever asked yourself: does your religion teach you to always love with actions and not just words, to be patient in your approach and to give with peace in your heart? If not, then you must re-evaluate what is being engrained in your psyche by your religious leader. All religions were created to be the pathway to the Creator and never to be used as a form of human indoctrination *and/or* manipulation. You should always accept and align the word of God with your spirit. If you are genuine in your walk, then religious exclusion should never be in your daily prayers and practices. Most people claim that their religion is the *true religion*, which has the ability to direct many souls back to God's paradise. Yet their actions on earth are far from holy. Wars are waged in the name of the *holy one* (from all religions) because they all believe that they are fighting for the preservation of their *own* beliefs. But whose opinion can be interpreted as the actual truth and why should we to believe their endless claims? From generation to generation, humanity has been decimated in order for some to prove that their *specific* religion is the only one that is God sent. Correct me if I am wrong, but does it not teach (in all holy books) about the importance of kindness, the acceptance of those who are in need and the emphasis to love *all* people; as God loved us all? Let us all lean towards the inclusion of all people, regardless of any difference or belief that has kept us apart in the past. Let us vehemently shun gossip and judgments, embrace diversity and equality because we are all the same in the eye of the Creator. We are all individually beautiful, brilliant and gifted with genius talent. Let us not pray and worship daily, to only turn and speak negatively of others. Let us understand and accept that we all have a responsibility to take care of each other's souls; for what connects us is far greater than what separates us. Let us collectively fight for all people who may be oppressed throughout the globe. The goal in life is to evolve into an *accepting* being and reach heights that may seem unattainable to the unbeliever. Love must be the only religion on this planet. In order to become a *complete human being,* one must first free one's mind from society's expectations. You must *unlearn* what you have been taught throughout your life and accept all people as your equal; regardless of their religious beliefs. Know that acceptance is the only path to love and full freedom.

so…is it **INCLUSION or EXCLUSION**?

Do you ever stop and just watch the world move? I have a tendency to sometimes go to the beach and just quietly watch the ocean's waves for many hours. Mesmerized by its beauty and intrigued by its silent strength. I have also been known to sit in the park, watching birds fly about, staring at bees as they slowly descend onto flowers and admiring different people hurriedly going about their day. My reflections are not just visual, but also insightful to the wonders of life. Constantly marveling at random thoughts: such as the beauty of a baby developing within a mother's womb or mathematical equations that are solved for mankind to be able to fly to outer space. I am intrigued by the unspeakable pain that one can cause through the illusion of love; I marvel at the beauty of souls who fight for equality because they know that we are all equal under the watchful eye of our creator. I stand in awe of the struggles, lessons and experiences that have molded me into the human that I have been blessed to become. I am infinitely amazed by the brilliant minds of those who have the ability to do things that cause me great difficulty to comprehend. I know that we can't all be great at everything, but I also know that we are all individually brilliant in our own crafts. I have come to realize that God is in all things. It took me a long time to really understand and accept this truth. I know that *just because* we hear, doesn't mean that we listen. *Just because* we see, doesn't mean that we take in. *Just because* we touch, doesn't mean we fully feel. *Just because* we taste, doesn't mean that we savor. I have learned to slow down and take everything in, instead of rushing through life and not fully enjoying it. They say that everyone dies, but not everyone lives. So it is essential that one must learn to live and not just exist. Shun working one's entire life and only enjoying the last 10-15 years of life, after retirement. God is in everything and everyone, yet many choose to not accept this truth, due to our free will. We all have the right to live our lives however we choose to, but we must take responsibility for the choices that we make. Once we pay attention to the simple blessings that we may take for granted, life becomes more pleasurable. Never worry about what anyone says, just go by what you feel. Your intuition will never steer you wrong or give you any kind of false direction throughout your life. Complaining is a waste of energy and time; know that everyday is a new day. Tomorrow's challenges are still going to come, no matter how much you continually stress, yesterday's problems are a thing of the past and today is a present that is to be appreciated and endlessly savored. Remember that you were created to work hard and achieve great things in this world; but at the same time, you are to also enjoy the fruits of your labor. The blessings will always come; just be patient and embrace what God has already reserved for you.

know that...**GOD IS IN EVERYTHING**

HELP OTHERS

Chapter 7

What makes you happy? What brings joy to your soul? We have all heard the term: *life is too short*, so we should live our lives in whatever capacity that brings us infinite happiness. But life happens and at times we are thrown off our paths due to unpredictable events. Regardless of what comes to distract us, we must never lose sight of what we were put here to do. That passion, the love, the desire is forever burning in our hearts, regardless of how distracted we may become. We all know many people who give up on their dreams, disregard their talent and succumb to the negativity that the world never takes a break from spewing. Their impatience sows doubt as the indiscipline allows complacency to take over the fire that has always burned within them. Once this occurs, endless excuses become the norm, blame is placed on others and the soul slowly begins to fade away. You must remember that everyone *exists* and eventually *dies*, but not everyone *lives*; most are doubtful of the talent lying within them. We are all born with greatness, but many aren't courageous enough to reveal their gift to the world. Doing what we love will never feel like work or a chore. It will never cause us to complain about Mondays and only look toward the weekends. Doing what we love will alleviate stress; it will awaken the soul with a happiness that comes to brighten the world. Doing what you love will inspire others to chase their own dreams and *pay it forward* toward anyone that they come to encounter. You can't make a change or leave a mark in this world if you don't follow your own path and try to emulate anyone else. It is great to be inspired by others, but make sure that the road you choose to walk will only have your name on it. Make sure to never make the mistake of wanting to be like anyone else. You are unique, beautiful, gifted and most importantly as talented as anyone that you may come to admire in your lifetime. It does not matter how long it takes you to reach your goals and dreams, the important factor is to never give up and always bring others along your successful journey. You are here to create, innovate and help others do the same. Focusing on admiration and wealth will only derail your journey. Humility and openness with the masses will bring you greater riches throughout your life. So don't worry about working towards gaining a profession, but focus on reaching your dreams and doing what makes you happy. Before this day ends, I want you to look within and ask yourself if you are willing to overcome the tests of life and achieve what has always sat in your spirit. Your happiness, your life and your peace of mind depends on the choices that you choose to make after you finish reading this passage.

SO...**DO WHAT MAKES YOU HAPPY**

There are many of us in this world who suffer from a condition which causes us to blindly offer our hearts to others, without any reservation. We seek out the best in people and hope that they have the decency to care for the fragility of our emotions. We tend to disregard their inability to care for our kindness, as they only seek to prey on the openness of our hearts. Many say that we are willfully at fault for the misuse of our affectionate ways; thus deserving of the pain caused by this blindness. Nonetheless we still seek to advance this world that is full of hate and bent on destruction by fools who have shunned love and all its beauties. We are all guilty of giving without taking into account the repercussions of it not being reciprocated. Eventually, all things that bring negative energy, must come to an end. The notion of being *used* by others to forward *their* own agenda shall no longer be tolerated. One can only take so much until one realizes that enough is enough. Sometimes we care too much for those who could care less about us; so at this point I hope that you make it a priority to stop being used. You were not put here to be anyone's rag doll or a toy to be mistreated in any way. Understand that whoever doesn't appreciate you, should no longer have access to you or the most precious thing that you can offer (your time). You were placed on this earth to be a guiding light to anyone that you come to encounter throughout your life's journey. You were created to be *used* for the glory of your Creator. Your talents and gifts are to be used for people to see the power that you were given to inspire. So you must be very careful as to who you allow to enter your space, who you give access to your time and what they bring to your existence. There is a sacred place in you that is supposed to be closed off to the world and only accessed by your Creator; so make sure that you are always available to help those in need. At birth you were given a gift called *intuition* (gut feeling) that will always guide you in the path that you choose to travel. Anything that comes to throw you off will always bring friction to your intuition; never disregard these internal messages that are sent to you on a daily basis. At this point I would like for you to examine everyone who has access to you and then determine if they are a positive or negative in your life. If they are a positive, then continue to build with them and inspiring one another. If they are a negative, then you must shed yourself of their presence; for they are only learning lessons and are to never to be viewed as a loss of time. Everyone who comes into your life comes with a purpose, so it is up to you to seek their hearts and see how long their season is meant to last. Allow no one to overstay their welcome because you always have a responsibility to stride forward and never dwell in what *would've, should've* or *could've* happened. God speed ahead, my friend.

so...**BE USED, NOT MISUSED!**

What is *your* inspiration in life? Better yet, what is your aspiration? Do you believe that your gift was solely given to you for the benefit of just attaining a *better* life for yourself? These are the types of questions that I tend to ask myself before I sit on any panel, give any interview *and/or* just have a simple conversation about life with an old friend. It is hard to not see oneself as an inspiration if one believes that *s/he* was put on this earth to inspire others and help them reach their own great potential. It is a gift, even though at times it may feel more like a curse. People will reach out to you and ask for your advice or just want to casually *pick* your brain. Nonetheless, take it as a compliment and know that you have something special that attracts them to you. Once you have found your gift (what you are great at), make sure that you do everything in your power to share it with the world. You must always aspire to inspire when you open your mouth, display your talent or offer them what you have been blessed with. You never know who is listening and is in need of your blessings. We never know what people are actually going through, so we must always attempt to be a light within the corners of the world's darkness. People will look up to you, even when you don't know that they admire you. Your voice is as powerful as any great person who has ever walked this earth. You were not created to be mediocre, nor were you created to shy away from the genius that you truly are. Your placement here was no mistake and you must understand this (and accept) in order to fulfill your destiny. Everything that you do or say on your path, will either encourage or discourage others; so be very careful with your words and your actions. Remember that no one knows their length of time on this earth; so cherish every minute and perfect your craft as much as you can.

You must put *more* time in working on your dreams, than you do at your day job. Those who are struggling will always look to you for guidance, so you must try to always inspire them with your own greatness. I know that it may be too much to ask of you, but I believe in you. I only tell you this because I know that you were born to lead. No matter what life continues to throw at you, know that you will always persevere because you are a leader, a warrior and a lover of all people. You are infinitely blessed because you love to see others succeed and achieve their own dreams. You don't envy, hate or gossip about others because you have been where they presently are. You know what it is to feel depressed, to feel empty and to feel that you are not where you thought you'd be in life. But you are more complete, strong and beautiful than you will ever know. So pick up that head of yours because they are all watching, regardless if you do well or if you fall on your face. Your response to them is solely up to you. Either you are going to be the brightness that they need to see or the darkness that they have been accustomed to. It is all up to you.

so... **ASPIRE TO INSPIRE**

There are many ways that we can support those in need; be it family members, friends or strangers. *Being there* for someone is an absolute blessing. Throughout my lifetime I have realized that the best way to support anyone who is constantly going through a challenge is merely to just genuinely *listen*. At times we can be overbearing because we want to do every and any thing to help. Of course it is done in good faith and with attempts to shield the person from whatever they are going through. Even though it may not be what they need at the time. We must learn to just sit down, listen, take it all in and do what is asked, rather than *jump the gun* and make things worse. Throughout our lives we have been conditioned to rush in and speak out, as we try to help alleviate someone's pain. So it is inherently within us to just speak and not fully listen. I have recently begun to make a valiant effort to stop trying to be the *savior* of all and just listen when a friend calls. I now understand that I may not be fully equipped to help all, but if I allow myself to just be quiet, then perhaps I can offer more help to them. The art of listening to understand, instead of listening to respond, is one feat that many of us have yet to perfect. But I understand, we usually respond without genuinely listening to the entire situation, because we all feel that we can prematurely contribute a solution to the problem. We feel that we may know the individual (well enough) that we can interrupt when they are just *venting*. We tend to interject by projecting our own personal experiences and then respond with how *we* would handle the issue, instead of just quietly listening. The true essence of a friendship purely rests on the ability and importance of being a good listener. It takes a lot to just sit back, take it all in and not respond without fully grasping the entirety of their issue. I will be the first to admit that it took me many years to understand this concept. See, most people are great at *just* hearing some things and responding right away. The impulse to respond overcomes the need to truly listen. There are many people going through tough times and they have *no one* to vent to or to just release the stress that is attempting to overcome their daily peace of mind. It can be very challenging to build one's courage to reveal oneself and tell others what is troubling them. Psychologists make a fortune off many who seek out their services. Psychologists rarely speak; they just sit there, observe, listen, take mental or physical notes and offer helping words when needed. People seek out psychologists because those in their personal circle lack the patience to just listen intently. Therefore they seek out a well paid stranger (whom they've never met) because many don't have the capability to be their *open ear*. I guarantee you that your *friend/family* member would rather sit and talk to you, instead of laying on someone's expensive couch and revealing what is truly bothering them. So in short, try being a better friend.

SO…**BE A GOOD LISTENER**

There is so much expected of you! In conception, we all came here with a purpose that is expected to be carried out. Circumstances come to test you, tribulations to derail you, pain to strengthen you and love to liberate you. But everything has its time and all things occur when they are supposed to. There are no coincidences in life, no mistakes and most importantly no losses. You will either win or you learn; it really is that simple. As you continue to make progress in your life, various responsibilities will come and you will always rise to the occasion. Understand that in life you will never be given a task that is too hard for you to overcome; everything takes time. Your blessings come with expectations. You are expected to not only bask in the glory of your success, but to also generously share your blessings onto others. Our world will always have difficulties and people will always seek the *blessed* ones for assistance. Your humility must always be in tact as you navigate through the endless expectations that come your way. You must remember how you overcame your past struggles, whenever it feels as if things are getting too hard to bear. Just think back to that old distraught, struggling, stressed and confused person that you used to be, well before your name became synonymous with prosperity, influence and success. Your upbringing was no coincidence, the scars of your early life were not losses and the choices you made molded you into the person you are today. No matter how well you are presently doing in life, know that we are all a work in progress. Regardless of how powerful your name rings throughout the corners of this beautiful earth, know that you were not exalted overnight. Every *praise* was paid for by the tears that you hid from the world and every autograph that you signed was paid for by someone who struggled before you and paved the road for you to walk on. These expectations are not of the world, but of the ONE who embedded that talent in you; which made the world exalt and magnify your name. Your presence and your voice will give hope to many who presently honor you and many who will come to speak of you. It may have taken you a while to get here, but remember that no dream or gift has an expiration date when it's on God's time. It will arrive when it is supposed to and when it does, you must use your gifts to better the world. You are required to spread blessings to all places that you are able to reach. Your gift must not be used exclusively, but openly for all to benefit from. Remember that you are expected to use every drop of your given talents before you are called to leave this earth. Note to self.

SO...**MUCH IS GIVEN, MUCH IS EXPECTED**

There is a gratitude which comes from helping to others, that can never be measured. Community work is a self-fulfilling action that is designed to bring inner love and a satisfaction that can not be bought. Community work is our way of giving back to those in need and taking the necessary time to share some of our blessings with others. If you have never participated in any kind of community work, you may want to connect with others who have. It is not to be done to glorify oneself, rather to inspire others to get involved as well. The greatest gift of being part of community work is the people that you meet and their powerful stories; especially the homeless. I have personally connected, cried, laughed and heard their stories as to how they became homeless. They are some of the most profound human beings, yet they find themselves in such precarious situations. It's not just about organizing a yearly thanksgiving dinner or just collecting winter items with your friends to disperse or strategizing toy drives to pass out to the communities in need. It is more than that; it is about physically touching the hands of strangers, conversing with them, engaging yourself and listening to understand the paths that they have traveled. Everyone has a great story to tell, you just have to be willing to listen. The greatest teacher on earth is one's personal experience. Personal experiences and the experiences of others will mold you into the great human being that you are meant to become and who the world will always remember you by. Affluence and power can make your life easier, but the relationships that are built are the most important factors. Many say that community work is a thankless job, but I beg to differ. It is the most unselfish act to perform in life. The ability to help others enhance their own lives is priceless. I know that we all deserve to live prosperous and stress free lives, yet we must all remember the responsibility of reaching back and helping out those who just need some assistance. Once again, I am compelled to remind you that everyone is fighting a daily battle (either if they show it or not), so your positive intervention can help lead them to their victory. We are all put here to help and inspire one another in any capacity. Selfishness is a disease that can only evolve if one feeds its ugly head. So let us generate greatness by helping out one another. There are many forms of community work which doesn't entail physical exertion; donating one's voice toward progression can also suffice. In other words, you don't have to be there, just help promote unity and those *field agents* will do all of the necessary work for the many who are in dire need of a helping hand.

COMMUNITY WORK

In our hearts, we were all given compassion. We all have the ability to connect with other beings on this planet because of the love, empathy and kindness that rests within us all. The question in hand is: when and how do we choose to exercise these virtues? We were all born with the gift (*free will*) to make our own decisions as to how we will live our lives and how we choose to treat others. I understand that there is much evil in the world and throughout your lifetime they will be many people who will try to *backstab* you and/or make you feel unappreciated. But somehow you must find a way to keep your heart clean, regardless of who comes to taint it. Find charities to donate to and if you can't afford to donate, find a way to give your time to make this a better world. When you give to a person or an organization, make sure that you are giving from the goodness of your heart. I know that sometimes you may want to feel appreciated and perhaps even recognized for your gestures of good faith, but what matters is that you are positively contributing to the progression of humanity. The universe (as they say) will reciprocate what you choose to put out into the world; so your selfless giving will never go unnoticed, even if you don't receive a conventional award from society. Friends and family will always ask for favors and if you decide to do it for them, do it with the intention that they are going to pay it forward. Your gift is to help people, in hopes that they will extend your generosity to others who may be in need. This life moves in circular motions, so when we give, we are willingly offering another being a piece of ourselves. If we expect something in return, then what we do is not done with a genuine heart. There is nothing worse than a complainer who believes that gossip is the best way to shame another person for revealing a blessing given to them. One must try to stay clear of *friends* and family members who always seek public credit for what they genuinely do for you. Unfortunately you will encounter these types of people, but your best option is to remain thankful for the great lesson gained in dealing with them. Your main goal is to keep your soul clean and remain open to helping anyone in need. At any given time you can become *the one* who may be in need of some assistance. Remember that your blessings come from the goodness that you do and from your generosity. Expectations are nothing but precursors to constant disappointments. So kindly open your heart and extend yourself as much as you can.

GIVING without **EXPECTING**

Comfort is the enemy of success. Comfort is the brother of complacency that can forever hold you from reaching the blessings that await you. In your journey, you must never allow yourself to feel as if you have *made it*. Every project that you attach yourself to, make sure to always attach the same passion in it as you did on your first project. You are only as good as your last success. No one wants to hear you brag about what you used to do and how you were so *great* and revered in the past. The greatest challenge (professionally) is to remain relevant and I have found the secret. It is simple: just be yourself and be real with those who surround you. Your refusal to reveal the expected work ethic of those around you can become your downfall. You must surround yourself with *go-getters* who despise *self-pity* and childish excuses. You have to push them to reach their greatest potential and in return they will inspire you as well. They say that iron sharpens iron; therefore you must always challenge one another to reach greater heights. This is the secret to staying sharp, relevant and determined on your path to greatness. Your reputation will always precede you, as society will always come to break you. You must remain steadfast in your beliefs and your convictions. This is the only way that you will inspire others to reach their own greatness. Remember that *they* eventually mimic what they see and never what they hear. Your own work ethic, focus and discipline will constantly be scrutinized, so you have a responsibility to repeatedly put forth your *greatest* work. But most importantly, you must remove those in your circle who are only there to benefit from your labor. Everyone must carry their own weight on the team. Nothing is given freely because freeloaders usually slow down the process; you have no time to lose. We all have a responsibility to make great use of our talents. If you are the leader, then everyone will look to you for guidance and inspiration. It is vital to always aspire to inspire; for if you become too comfortable, then those around you will also "take the foot off the pedal," sort of speak. It is okay to slow down from time to time, in order to relax the body and mind, but progression must continue on, even if it's a slow or a fast pace. You have to always keep moving. Remember that the world is always watching. There are many who came before you, whom were possibly nervous and perhaps shied away from their own opportunities. So remember to always give your heart, your pain, your struggles, you perseverance, tears and your smiles; but accept the fact that they may still speak negatively of you. Your life is a reflection of the efforts that you put in and the fears that you have overcome.

so…**NEVER** get too **COMFORTABLE**

LOVE

Chapter 8

Many have been known to say that freedom is the epitome of life. So what is love? Love is said to be the liberator of all and no one can fully survive this journey of life without its powerful potency. We all crave every great feeling that comes from love; the passion, the vulnerability and the warmth that it brings. Within, we all know and feel when it's real or when it is used as a weapon of deceit against us. They say that love is only complete when it is given without expectation, but I disagree. What is the point of giving without reciprocity? Personally it is my drug of choice, but I am careful with whom I share my love with. Blind love can leave lasting effects on the psyche and can also bring physical harm. Love has no color, no gender, no race, no religion and no preference. You can love who you want to love, without the expectation and influence of society. Society will never keep you warm at night, it will not comfort you when you have a bad day and it will definitely not come to your rescue in times of need. Love should never be separated by border walls or by the guilty expectations of family members. Negative projections of those closest to you have the possibility to sway you away from what God has in store for you; so be careful who you allow to whisper in your ears. We have been separated through the impotence of culture and the need to stay within the confines of personal comfort. We are all aware of the human comfort that comes from one's upbringing and the expectancy to stay within *your own* people. Most are manipulated through the guise of *love*, even though we are all one people under the Creator's eyes. The illusion of love can be used to manipulate masses into believing that love is not a necessity. Those who fear repercussion from *their own* race, will never know true freedom, nor the capacity which love entails. Love is the only entity in life that can free the soul from stress, anger, worries and emptiness. Love is gentle and has a beautiful and subtle way of making one forget all that *s/he* is struggling with. No matter how hard life becomes, love has the ability to bring a simple smile. Regardless of who comes to disrupt your inner peace, you must always reach out to others who willingly love you with no hesitation. Every single day, you must allocate free time to bask in the power of love; for the world's noises will always come to drown your peace. Words are great when speaking of love, but the action behind those words is what we all desire. Love is silent and need not be ever boasted for the world's approval. Just unabashedly show what you feel for your chosen one and *love* will do the rest.

LOVE IS FREEDOM

There is a big difference between being *alone* and being *lonely*. Life is about relationships and the bonds created between people; which sometimes don't work out. The pain of breaking up can at times be too much to bear for some. It has the potential to lead to depression and it can also subject one to become more reclusive and introvert. Understand that it's okay to step back from the world and take some free time to heal. It is also okay to be alone and patiently allow your personal growth to take its course, after experiencing such trauma. That is the importance of being alone and allowing self-reflection to heal one's soul. But one must be careful to not allow loneliness to creep in. Loneliness welcomes the necessity of companionship and the *need* to belong to something or someone. Being lonely can make one susceptible to becoming easy prey for those who are seeking to pounce on such vulnerabilities. The necessity to have another human being in one's life is a dangerous path to tread. This can easily lure *you* into becoming just a point of interest for a few simple nightly rendezvous and of course the early morning disappearances. How you are valued will always depend on the price you project for yourself unto the world. You can't expect respect and equal treatment when you display the opposite. One must be extremely cautious with the conversations that one has with their person of interest. Your weakness can easily be exposed and then exploited when you offer your love out of *necessity*. This has the potential to occur after a bad separation or from the accumulation of past hurts. Understand that if you are not fully healed from your past relationships, you will continue to hurt others and remain an open invite to also be hurt. Many like to say that *one should take a chance* with love and have no expectations; all while disregarding the vicious cycle of unchecked residual pains. Self awareness and self-evaluations are vital when one decides to open up to love *again* and the possibility of its blessings. We are all guilty of stepping into relationships, fully aware that our healing process may not be fully completed. But age and maturity only brings forth knowledge to those who heed the lessons of their painful pasts. If the lessons are not properly observed, then the same mistakes will continue to plague one's heart and disrupt the mind. This is why most people make their choices through emotions and lust, while excusing the actions of those who are in their lives for a season and not for a worthy reason.

so...**NEVER LOVE OUT OF NECESSITY**

If you are going to give, make sure you give everything or nothing. There is no point in entering a relationship if you are going to hesitate with your heart, soul and spirit. If you are afraid to get hurt, you don't feel like sacrificing and are unwilling to communicate when problems arise, then don't waste your time and definitely do not waste the other person's time either. Love is the most beautiful thing that you can experience in life, but toying with it is highly disrespectful to your creator and the one who's willing to meet you halfway. I have been guilty of such discretions because companionship and relationship can at times create blurred lines when one is not fully ready to commit. You do not need a self-proclaimed *love guru* to explain the responsibilities and/or expectations of the love that you feel within. The question is: are you willing to share it with all? Availability requires transparency and vulnerability. If you are guarded, due to previous negative experiences with love, then you not ready for a relationship. Freedom from all must be achieved for one to openly embrace the infinite possibilities of love. So you must ask yourself: have I gotten over the one(s) who hurt me in the past and caused me to curse love? You must be fully honest with yourself because if you're not then you will subconsciously and inadvertently project your own pain onto others. You do not have the right to choose to only offer some parts of yourself and hide others under the guise of protecting your *heart* from a possible heartbreak. That kind of selfishness will cause unnecessary pain to others, when you are unwilling to be transparent with them and yourself. Love is easily and effortlessly given when the heart knows that it has found a worthy connection. We can not chase love, pay for love, change ourselves for love and in return expect the outcome to be mutual. You must always be yourself;

eventually the one who is meant for you will be aligned with you. So promptly put a stop to these frivolous, time consuming, unfulfilling and dead-end relationships that you know are not going anywhere. Comfort must never be used as an excuse to remain in a state of misery. *True love* is immune to any negativity. Know your worth and know when that time comes when you must walk away. You must remove yourself from any relationship that lacks mental *stimulation,* passionate *fixations,* intriguing *conversations* and daily *transformations.* Love is meant to enhance your life and vice versa. Anything less is unworthy.

it's...**EVERYTHING or NOTHING**

What are past relationships good for? Should you try to work out anything with an *ex* that may still have a piece of your heart? It's a simple answer: NO! He or she is an *ex* for a reason. The pain they caused you in the past, can not and will not ever change anything between you two; presently or in the future. We are all guilty of attempting to *work out* a relationship that may have gone sour. But in the long run the *resurrected* relationship is never what either one of you expect it to be. The arguments return, the expectations are never met and the love rests on a comfort zone that is based on a past connection between both individuals. Once someone shows you who they really are, you must do yourself a favor and accept them for nothing more. Any attempts to change a person or have any false hopes that they'll conform to whom you want them to be, will always backfire. Your evaluation of yourself should never be based on how others love you. Self esteem, self love and self respect should always be enough to sustain you, especially when past interests attempt to resurface. There is no loss in any relationship that didn't work out; in all actuality it offers the opposite. The lessons learned are invaluable, as you gain a more vivid comprehension of yourself and what you vowed to never allow again. In all honesty, the lack of reciprocity in love is one of the greatest pains that one may ever experience. Those who have been in love and heartbroken before, know that it takes a *very long time* to recover from such anguish. Nonetheless, you must never allow yourself to return to *the one* who caused you much heartache. Any excuse made, for any individual who hurts you, is the greatest disrespect to the self. Stop allowing others to pillage your heart and your sacred body; eventually they will depart from your life *again*. Remember that every action that you excuse will always be used against you, as they re-attempt to regain access to your most sacred treasures. You must, at all costs, learn to protect your love, your mind, your body and your spirit against anyone who does not have your best interests at heart. Backtracking will only deter your progression and put a hold on your blessings. You must always know that the comfort of the *past* is the enemy of the *future*, while you sit still in the *present*, trying to figure out why you're still hurting. Aren't you *tired* of being sick and tired? Just let go and let God.

so...**LET THE PAST GO**

They say that in every relationship, one person has the control and the other just follows along. Usually this is determined by the percentage of love that is given and received by both individuals in the relationship. We all know someone (if not ourselves) who does all of the chasing, while the other half shows minimal effort and receives all of the benefits of love. The pain which causes endless tears, the constant screaming/arguing due to un-reciprocated love, the accepted excuses because one can't see oneself without the other person. Never accept the lesser role in your relationship because you feel that *the love* is too great to let go. Never consciously disregard the self and remain fearful to project one's self-worth to a partner who *claims* to infinitely love you. You must stare into the mirror, eyes balled out from the endless tears as you barely hang on to your sanity, and ask yourself if you've shown yourself to be worthy of a love that you require? You've been knocked down so much (from different relationships) that you no longer know what you deserve. You accept the taunting of your heart, the disrespect of your being and the open neglect which has been normalized, due to your loss of self control. Basking in the oceans of pity, you willingly lie on a bed of misery that is created by others; yet your screams remain hollow and your demands are *undemanding*. This is why you are controlled by love; this is why you *accept* everything that you receive, even though within your being, you know that you deserve much more. But you have a *type* and that certain *type* has always been your weakness. You eventually become consumed by lust and destroyed by experiences that you refuse to accept and learn from. You are blindly chasing love within a dark soul, who may also be lost. So how do you find a love that will not control you, but instead liberate you? Simple...stop looking outside of your own being. Every single thing that you have ever attempted to find (in love), has always lied within the beauty that remains hidden in you. Love is an inside job, not an outer inheritance. Anyone who comes into your life has a responsibility to enhance what you were born with; if not, then you are to part ways until you feel the opposite and receive what you deserve. Love is meant to be given freely and not used as a source of control. You have a duty to protect everything that God blessed you with and you must never allow any other human being to strip you of that kind of love. Chase no one, beg no one, plead with no one to love you properly and under no circumstances belittle yourself for anyone who does not know how to treat you correctly. You know exactly how you deserved to be loved!

so...**DON'T BE CONTROLLED BY LOVE**

We have all been in this situation before! Love is a powerful aphrodisiac and it has the strength to shatter the heart, if it is not reciprocated. Once one falls deeply in love, one's soulful, mental, emotional, physical and spiritual connection with the other being is indescribable. This bond is something that we all yearn for, but also fear that it may have total control over us. I believe that humanity is unable to survive without love and its ability to connect us with our creator. I have experienced (as many others have) the struggles of love and had my heart shattered when it was not reciprocated with an equal dose of passion and consistency. The fear that comes (after such an experience) can be piercing and traumatizing to one's psyche. Nevertheless I have come to realize that time is the greatest healer of a broken heart. There is nothing to be said, nor done for the heart when it begins its healing; one must just allow the process to take its course. It may feel as if you will not make it, that you'll crack under pressure and be unable to overcome your time of brokenness. I will not lie to you, it's not easy and it will test your inner strength as nothing has before. Yet you must believe that you will be alright and you will get through the struggle because something greater always comes. There is no time limit or expectation for how long the healing process should take, but you must know that nothing lasts forever. Slowly allow love to flourish again, as you continue to heal. We were all put on this earth to be consumed by what many refer to as a *true love*. A love that is mutual between two beings. Until you are engulfed by this type of love, you must continue to patiently wait on it. You must not allow the bitterness of your past or the fear of rejection and pain to take away you ability to open up your heart again. I understand that you are scared of being hurt again, but you must believe that God will bring you through your struggles and bless you with a love like never imagined. You must show your ability and capability to love again; it will inspire others to do the same. I have finally understood that no matter the amount of success attained, the riches that one acquires or the notoriety that one receives, none can ever compare to what love brings. To reach one's dream and not have anyone to share it with in life, is the ultimate tragedy. Remember that you were given a spirit of love to give and receive.

YOU'VE BEEN HURT, TRY AGAIN

Many have been known to say that one must always display one's love for their other half. This may be done for various reasons: to satisfy the other mate or to reassure them that you feel the same as they do about you. But many people have uttered this powerful word and numerously hurt the ones who they claim to have loved. The *word* love has been misused to receive favors, to manipulate others and to be used as one's crutch when one is in trouble. Love is the greatest gift offered to mankind, but most of us have defiled it and used it as a form of manipulation. I must say that I am equally guilty, so I don't exempt myself from taking responsibility for my previous misuse of *love*. I have come to realize that love is more than what we say; it is what we consistently do. Love is gazing at the one that you choose to share your life with and constantly pray for nothing but happiness for them. But know that there will be times that you both may not see *eye to eye*. Love is accepting someone and *showing* them that you put them above any other who comes to destroy your union. Love is cooking a meal, setting the table and opening the door before your mate walks in, because you are aware of the *hectic days* that they usually have at work. Love is sending a quick message with hopes that they have a great day. Love is picking out her favorite flowers or rubbing his back because he was just laid-off from his job. Love is allowing her to cry in your arms when she's in need, even though she is the boss at her job. Love is supporting and helping one another achieve a joint dream without bitterness or jealousy. Love is the understanding that two people are *equally* and *willingly* contributing to each other's happiness, joy, success and knowing that you always have each other's best interests at heart; even when others say that you are too *lovey-dovey* together.

Love is closing your eyes and feeling your mate run their fingers down your face, tracing the wrinkles of your beautiful smile. Many have become *too cool* to display love; which eventually leads to a premature separation. Don't ever be that *too cool* kind of person. People miss out on the greatest experiences in life because they are too busy with trying to impress others and claim that they are content with being alone. No one was created to be alone in this world; we have all been assigned a partner in life. That specific partner is the one who can not be without you and always calls to check on your well-being. This partner is always concerned about your health, your peace of mind and your happiness. They constantly ask if you have eaten, remind you to reach your destination safely and always want to hear your voice before going to sleep. Love is the genuine act of being patient and knowing that it does not need to be screamed from mountain tops. We all want to be told that we are loved, but it is more important to just feel that genuine love from others.

LOVE IS IN THE ACTIONS
NOT JUST THE WORDS

Love is said to be similar to anything that is meant to be savored and enjoyed. Most of us rush into it and expect it to be everlasting. But love can not and must not ever be hurried or placed on any pedestal or expectation. Love must be what it was created to be; a masterpiece while mastering peace. Many get lost in the *honeymoon stage* because they are unable to have self-restraint when it comes to the overwhelming feeling of love. I say this because I have also been guilty of this in the past. It is hard to hold back and fight it at the same time; especially when it is experienced for the first time. I have learned to just walk rather than run, wait instead of chasing and to listen before speaking. Time brings wisdom and love is the greatest teacher one can ever have in this life. It is an acquired skill that is attained through patience and time. I understand that the heart wants what it wants and when it wants it, but the mind serves as the mediator that brings balance to the excitement of love. Once you learn to take your time and enjoy every moment of love, then you commence your true journey towards the path of happiness and a soulful peace. If one chooses to rush love, then jealousy, envy and insecurities have the ability to disrupt such a bond between two human beings. There should never be any competition between two partners, when it comes to love. Love is kind and subtle, not boastful and controlling. Love can only be accepted and enjoyed if it's genuinely given and received freely without any terms, expectations or stipulations. It can not be forced or used as a form of control. In order to truly enjoy the beauty of love, one must be patient and never question where the love may lead. One must understand that there is no limit or end to love; so just pace yourself. Love has the ability to alleviate the stress that is caused by the world's endless expectations. Love can help you live longer and consume you like nothing else will in life. You don't have to speak on it or show it off in any way because the world will see that you are glowing with its light. You awake with a different smile, speak with great confidence and sing a different tune. Being in love is perhaps the greatest and most satisfying period of one's life. Nothing or no one should ever have the ability to take that feeling away from you, so hold it close. You must bask in it, speak life into it, live in it, dance in it and most importantly take your time and breathe the daily blessing that comes from the beauty of it. This is *love*. This is your met*amor*phosis.

so...**TAKE YOUR TIME** & **ENJOY EVERY MOMENT**

If there is no struggle, there is no progress.
Those who profess to favor freedom, and yet
depreciate struggle, are men who want crops
without plowing up the ground.

-Frederick Douglass

metAMORphosis

.Custodio Gomes.